DAVID MARSHALL LANG'S JOURNEY FROM RUSSIA TO ARMENIA VIA CAUCASIAN GEORGIA

Volume 2

THE BALAVARIANI

THE BALAVARIANI
Barlaam and Josaphat: A Tale from the Christian East

Edited by
DAVID MARSHALL LANG

Taylor & Francis Group
LONDON AND NEW YORK

First published in English in 1966 by George Allen & Unwin Ltd.

This edition first published in 2022
by Routledge
2 Park Square, Milton Park, Abingdon, Oxon OX14 4RN

and by Routledge
605 Third Avenue, New York, NY 10158

Routledge is an imprint of the Taylor & Francis Group, an informa business

© 1966 UNESCO. © English Translation David Marshall Lang.

All rights reserved. No part of this book may be reprinted or reproduced or utilised in any form or by any electronic, mechanical, or other means, now known or hereafter invented, including photocopying and recording, or in any information storage or retrieval system, without permission in writing from the publishers.

Trademark notice: Product or corporate names may be trademarks or registered trademarks, and are used only for identification and explanation without intent to infringe.

British Library Cataloguing in Publication Data
A catalogue record for this book is available from the British Library

ISBN: 978-1-03-215852-5 (Set)
ISBN: 978-1-00-325111-8 (Set) (ebk)
ISBN: 978-1-03-216861-6 (Volume 2) (hbk)
ISBN: 978-1-03-216870-8 (Volume 2) (pbk)
ISBN: 978-1-00-325070-8 (Volume 2) (ebk)

DOI: 10.4324/9781003250708

Publisher's Note
The publisher has gone to great lengths to ensure the quality of this reprint but points out that some imperfections in the original copies may be apparent.

Disclaimer
The publisher has made every effort to trace copyright holders and would welcome correspondence from those they have been unable to trace.

THE BALAVARIANI

(BARLAAM AND JOSAPHAT)

A TALE FROM THE CHRISTIAN EAST
TRANSLATED FROM THE OLD GEORGIAN

BY

DAVID MARSHALL LANG
Professor of Caucasian Studies
University of London

INTRODUCTION BY
ILIA V. ABULADZE
Director, Institute of Manuscripts
Georgian Academy of Sciences, Tbilisi

London
GEORGE ALLEN & UNWIN LTD
RUSKIN HOUSE   MUSEUM STREET

FIRST PUBLISHED IN 1966

This book is copyright under the Berne Convention. Apart from any fair dealing for the purpose of private study, research, criticism or review, as permitted under the Copyright Act, 1956, no portion may be reproduced by any process without written permission. Inquiries should be made to the publishers.

© UNESCO, 1966

UNESCO COLLECTION OF REPRESENTATIVE WORKS

SERIES OF TRANSLATIONS FROM THE
LITERATURES OF THE UNION OF SOVIET SOCIALIST
REPUBLICS

This work from the Georgian has been accepted in
the series of translations sponsored by the United Nations
Educational, Scientific and Cultural Organisation
in consultation with the Commission of the USSR for UNESCO
and the International Council for Philosophy and Humanist Studies

PRINTED IN GREAT BRITAIN
in 11 point Juliana type
BY THE BLACKFRIARS PRESS LTD
LEICESTER

BARLAAM AND JOSAPHAT

Was Barlaam truly Josaphat,
    And Buddha truly each?
What better parable than that
    The unity to preach—

The simple brotherhood of souls
    That seek the highest good;
He who in kingly chariot rolls,
    Or wears the hermit's hood!

The Church mistook? These heathen once
    Among her Saints to range!
That deed of some diviner dunce
    Our wisdom would not change.

For Culture's Pantheon they grace
    In catholic array.
Each Saint hath had his hour and place,
    But now 'tis All Saints' Day.

                      ISRAEL ZANGWILL
October 27, 1895   (1864-1926)

PREFACE

In the literary world of mediaeval Christendom, few worthies were more celebrated than the Indian hermit Barlaam and his royal pupil Prince Josaphat, who were supposed between them to have converted India to Christianity at some vaguely defined period of historical antiquity. The Churches celebrated their festival days with appropriate solemnity, and their relics were invested with exceptional healing power. In 1571, for instance, the Doge of Venice presented King Sebastian of Portugal with what purported to be a bone and part of the spine of St Josaphat, which later found their way to the cloister of St Salvator in Antwerp. Shakespeare adapted one of the holy Barlaam's fables for the episode of the Three Caskets in *The Merchant of Venice*, while Jesuit priests made the story the subject of edifying morality plays.

The practical influence of the story of Barlaam and Josaphat is inestimable, extending over many centuries and many countries. Its advocacy of the ascetic way of life and renunciation of the world inspired the mediaeval Albigensian heretics, to such an extent that the work has sometimes been taken to be a Cathar document. Equally striking is the story's impact on the great Leo Tolstoy, as recounted in his own *Confession*. Among the influences which determined Tolstoy to turn his back on wealth, fame and even his own family, that of the Buddha's Great Renunciation was among the most compelling. Not only does Tolstoy relate in his *Confession* some of the episodes of the Bodhisattva Prince's Renunciation, including the Four Omens, but he even quotes verbatim from the book of Barlaam and Josaphat one of the most effective of the fables whereby Barlaam (Balahvar in the Georgian text) seeks to demonstrate the valueless nature of human life on earth.

'There is an Eastern fable, told long ago, of a traveller overtaken on a plain by an enraged beast. Escaping from the beast he gets into a dry well, but sees at the bottom of the well a dragon that has opened its jaws to engulf him. And the unfortunate man, not daring to climb out lest he should be destroyed by the enraged beast, and not daring to leap to the bottom of the well lest he should be swallowed by the dragon, seizes a twig growing in a crack in the well and clings to it. His hands are growing weaker and he feels he will soon have to resign himself to the destruction that awaits him above or below, but still he clings on. Then he sees that two mice, one black and the other white, go regularly round and round the stalk to which he is clinging and gnaw at it. And soon the twig itself will snap and he will fall into the dragon's jaws.

'The traveller sees this and knows that he must inevitably perish: but while still hanging he looks around, sees some drops of honey on the leaves of the twig, reaches them with his tongue and licks at them.—So I too clung to the twig of life, knowing that the dragon of death was inexorably awaiting me, ready to tear me to pieces: and I could not understand why I had fallen into such torment. I tried to lick the honey which formerly consoled me, but the honey no longer gave me pleasure, and the white and black mice of day and night gnawed at the branch by which I hung. I saw the dragon clearly and the honey no longer tasted sweet. I only saw the dragon from which there was no escape, and the mice, and I could not tear my gaze from them. And this is not a fable, but the real unanswerable truth, intelligible to all!'

I must here express thanks to my Californian friend Mr Tom Foley, who drew this remarkable passage to my attention: the full text of the fable, taken from the Old Georgian version, appears on pages 77-78 of the present volume.

In spite of striking similarities between the pious career of St Josaphat and the traditional lives of Gautama Buddha, it was not until a century ago that the authenticity of this Christian cult was challenged, and definite proof produced to show that Barlaam and Josaphat were not early Christian saints at all, but legendary figures whose image was based on ancient Indian stories about the Bodhisattva prince and his Great Renunciation. Since that time, a large number of articles and books have been devoted to comparative study and analysis of the many versions of the Barlaam and Josaphat story which survive in virtually all

PREFACE

countries of Christendom from Iceland to Ethiopia, from Poland to the Philippines. Even today, traces of the legend crop up in unexpected places. For example, the Ahmadi sect in Islam have created a legend that a certain holy man named Yūz Āsaf, whom they identify with Our Lord Jesus Christ, came to Kashmir and died there; in reality, the whole Ahmadi story of 'Yūz Āsaf', as I have tried to show in a previous study, is simply based on an extract from the familiar Arabic version of the Barlaam and Josaphat romance, and has no connection with the life of Jesus Christ at all.[1]

In face of all this evidence of the diffusion of the Buddha's legendary life story and spiritual heritage throughout Christendom by the medium of the Barlaam and Josaphat legend, it is surprising to find writers on comparative religion who continue to devote entire volumes to listing the coincidental resemblances between Buddhism and Christianity, but without making any reference to Barlaam and Josaphat whatever.[2]

We should always bear in mind that the Barlaam and Josaphat romance is not a direct translation of any Indian original, but represents the result of a long migration of the life story and teaching of the Buddha through several different religious and cultural environments, until the work took on its final Christian shape and colouring. A particularly important role in this migration was played by the Manichaeans of Central Asia, and Arabic writers of Baghdad in the epoch of Harun al-Rashid. I have myself attempted to trace these eastern origins of the Barlaam and Josaphat legend in some separate articles, listed in the bibliography at the end of this volume, as well as in the introduction to my earlier book, *The Wisdom of Balahvar: A Christian Legend of the Buddha* (London: George Allen & Unwin; New York: The Macmillan Company, 1957). This work aroused interest in several countries; comments and suggestions were made which have been taken into account in the preparation of this new translation. However, no new evidence has been produced which would alter the main lines of my conclusions

[1] D. M. Lang, *The Wisdom of Balahvar: A Christian Legend of the Buddha*, London, Allen & Unwin, 1957, Postscript, pp. 129-30: 'Mr Graves, Mr Podro and the Kashmir Shrine'.

[2] The latest work of this category is Winston L. King's *Buddhism and Christianity. Some Bridges of Understanding*, London, Allen & Unwin, 1963.

relating to the tale's transmission through Central Asia, the Arab world, and the Caucasus. Indeed, these conclusions have been strongly confirmed by the remarkable discovery by Professor W. B. Henning and Dr Mary Boyce of two ancient manuscript fragments, bearing extracts of a Persian poetic version of the story of Bilauhar and Būdisaf (Barlaam and Josaphat), which bids fair to be the most venerable specimen of Classical Persian poetry known to us. Professor Henning has also drawn attention to the Manichaean ideas reflected in Bilauhar's teachings about prophets and their role in the revelation of eternal truth, as contained in the Arabic versions and faithfully reflected in the Christian Georgian adaptation.[1] (See particularly chapter 22 of the text, below.)

It is one of the many remarkable features of the Barlaam and Josaphat legend that one of the vital links in its passage from East to West is to be sought in the literary world of mediaeval Georgia, a Christian kingdom in the Caucasus which had served since the fourth century as a bastion of Christendom among the Infidels. The Georgians, who took the story direct from the Arabs, were apparently the first to give it a specifically Christian flavour. Theirs was the first Christian Church to include St Iodasaph—in reality the Bodhisattva prince of India—in the number of its saints and celebrate his festival with hymns and anthems, dating back to the tenth and eleventh centuries. But for the existence of this Georgian version, and the translation work of St Euthymius the Georgian (955-1028) on Mount Athos, the story might never have been rendered into Greek at all, nor reached the readers who enjoyed it in so many of the other tongues of mediaeval Christendom.

The authorities of UNESCO have now included this Georgian version of the legend of Barlaam and Josaphat in their series of translations of classic works from the literatures of non-Russian nations of the Soviet Union. The text used is the new and much more complete version discovered in manuscript form in Jerusalem and edited in 1957 by my colleague Ilia Abuladze, Director of the Institute of Manuscripts of the Academy of Sciences of the Georgian S.S.R., Tbilisi. Professor Abuladze has been engaged

---

[1] See W. B. Henning, 'Persian poetical manuscripts from the time of Rudaki', in A Locust's Leg: Studies in honour of S. H. Taqizadeh, London, 1962, pp. 89-98.

PREFACE

for many years in the study of the Georgian Barlaam and Josaphat romance and produced a critical edition of the abridged version, known as *The Wisdom of Balahvar*, as long ago as 1937. He was the first among Soviet scholars to evaluate the true significance of the new Jerusalem text, on which he worked for a time independently of myself. A Russian translation of the book, published at Tbilisi in 1962, was edited by him. He has now contributed a prefatory essay for this English translation; this essay I have translated into English with a few slight modifications for the benefit of English-speaking readers. I also have to thank Professor Gérard Garitte of the University of Louvain who checked the work carefully in typescript and pointed out several errors and omissions.

It is a source of deep personal pleasure to me that Ilia Abuladze and I have now been enabled to join forces in presenting to the Western public a work which illustrates to a unique degree the many common features which exist in Buddhism and Christianity, as well as throwing light on the evolution of asceticism and ascetic ideals among the Manichaeans, the Arabs and the Byzantine and Georgian Christians.

While this book was already in the press, news was received from Soviet Georgia of the recovery of yet another manuscript version of the Georgian *Balavariani*, this time in verse. The new text was found quite by chance in the Ratcha district, hidden in the trunk of a venerable yew tree, and has been described by Professor Giorgi Tsereteli in volume 108 of the Works of Tbilisi State University. The manuscript is relatively modern, dating from the eighteenth century, and adds little to our knowledge of the text. But the discovery is valuable as further evidence of the vitality and wide appeal of this truly remarkable story.

DAVID MARSHALL LANG

School of Oriental and African Studies
University of London
London, W.C.1

CONTENTS

PREFACE · *page* 9

INTRODUCTION
The Origins and History of 'Balavariani' and its Place among the Treasures of World Literature · · · · · · · 19

A HYMN TO THE BLESSED IODASAPH · · · · · · · · · · · · · · · · 43

BALAVARIANI
OR THE STORY OF BARLAAM AND JOSAPHAT

BOOK I: The Life of the Blessed Iodasaph, Son of Abenes, King of India, whom the Blessed Father and Teacher Balahvar converted · 53

BOOK II: Concerning the Arrival of our Holy and Blessed Father Balahvar, who converted the King's Son to the Religion of Christ · 71

Fable the First: The Trumpet of Death: The Four Caskets · · 73
Fable the Second: The Sower · 76
Fable the Third: The Man and the Elephant · · · · · · · · · · · · · · 77
Fable the Fourth: The Man and his Three Friends · · · · · · · · 78
Fable the Fifth: The King for One Year · 81
Fable the Sixth: Dogs and Carrion · 83
Fable the Seventh: Physician and Patient · · · · · · · · · · · · · · · · · · 84
Fable the Eighth: The Sun of Wisdom · 86
Fable the Ninth: The King and the Happy Poor Couple · · 90
Fable the Tenth: The Rich Youth and the Poor Maiden · · 93
Fable the Eleventh: The Fowler and the Nightingale · · · · · · 96
Fable the Twelfth: The Tame Gazelle · 112
Fable the Thirteenth: The Costume of Enemies · · · · · · · · · · · · 115

CONTENTS

BOOK III: *The Life and Ministry of the Blessed Iodasaph, the King's Son, whom the Holy Father Balahvar converted, and who converted his father King Abenes and the Land of India to the Service of Christ*   121

Fable the Fourteenth: *The Amorous Wife*   142

Fable the Fifteenth: *The Youth who had never seen a Woman*   144

SELECT BIBLIOGRAPHY AND NOTES FOR FURTHER READING   181

INDEX   185

ILLUSTRATIONS

I   Iodasaph meets the old man   *facing page* 80
    Balahvar reveals himself to Iodasaph

II   The Trumpet of Death   81
    The Fable of the Four Caskets
    The Man and the Unicorn

III   The Nightingale and the bird catcher   96
    The Baptism of Iodasaph
    King Abenes and the Ascetics

IV   Theudas acknowledging Christ   97
    Iodasaph in the desert

ACKNOWLEDGEMENTS

All but three of the illustrations are from a Greek manuscript, Iviron 463, preserved on Mount Athos. The picture of the Man and the Unicorn is from Greek Ms. 338 of King's College, Cambridge; note that the Unicorn here replaces the Elephant, which features in Fable 3 of the Georgian version. These photographs were generously supplied by Professor Sirarpie Der Nersessian, author of an important work on the illustrations of the Barlaam romance, by kind courtesy of the Collection chrétienne et byzantine of the École des Hautes Études, Paris.

The pictures of Balahvar revealing himself to Iodasaph, and King Abenes and the Ascetics, are taken from a Christian Arabic manuscript, No. B5/5 of the Monastery of Deir al-Shir, 15 miles from Beirut, Lebanon. These were first published by Father Jules Leroy in the journal *Syria*, 1955, and are reproduced here by his kind permission.

The photograph on the dust jacket shows the eleventh century church of Nikordsminda, in the Ratcha district of Georgia, and was kindly supplied by Professor V. Beridze of Tbilisi, to whom thanks are expressed.

INTRODUCTION

THE ORIGINS AND HISTORY OF 'BALAVARIANI' AND ITS PLACE AMONG THE TREASURES OF WORLD LITERATURE

1. THE EVOLUTION AND DIFFUSION OF 'BALAVARIANI'

'Balavariani' is the Georgian name for the extremely popular early mediaeval work which circulated widely in the East and in the West, and is known in Greek literature under the title 'The Life of Barlaam and Ioasaph'.[1] This hagiographical work relates the feats of its two main heroes, Barlaam and Ioasaph (in Georgian: Balahvar and Iodasaph), and their efforts in the cause of India's conversion to Christianity.

Many works of hagiography tell the story of champions of the Christian religion who lived at a definite point of time, and in concrete historical circumstances. Such works usually possess a definite value for the study of the history of a given country. However, when we come to examine *Balavariani* from this standpoint, we discover that the history of India contains no such description of the country's conversion to Christianity as that given in our narrative. A detailed study of the romance shows that it is based on a freely adapted version of one of the accounts of the legendary life story of the Buddha[2]—a book created within India itself. Consequently, before taking on the aspect of a work of hagiography, our *Balavariani* had a long path to travel.

It was no mere coincidence which led to the selection of a particular version of the life story of the Buddha, probably the *Lalita-vistara*, for adaptation in the form of a work of hagiography

---

[1] First published at Paris in 1832 by J. F. Boissonade, *Anecdota Graeca*, tom. IV. From this edition, it was reprinted in Migne, *Patrologia Graeca*, tom. XCVI, pp. 859-1240, and also in the Loeb Classical Library, London, New York, 1914.

[2] See *Istoriya russkoi literatury* ('History of Russian literature'), tom. I (Literature of the tenth to eighteenth centuries), compiled and edited by the Academy of Sciences of the USSR, 1958, p. 39.

after it had already passed through various different cultural, religious and social environments. The selection of such a source as the basis for a work of Christian literature was justified by the fact that the life and teaching of the Buddha have a number of points of resemblance to the life and teaching of Christ.

Before being recast as a work of hagiography, the Indian legend went through several phases of evolution. With the discovery of several episodes and fables in Manichaean manuscript fragments from Central Asia (written in Iranian and Old Turkish), it has become an established fact that the Buddha legend was well known in Iran. In this new environment, it must indisputably have undergone fresh modification.

It has been conjectured that in the next stage, at the period of the Iranian renaissance under King Khusrau Anushirvan (531-79), the legend was readapted in the Pehlevi language. In support of this, scholars have cited allusions and references in Arabic books of a later period, as well as translations into other languages possibly made from this lost version.[1] It has also been conjectured that at this same period, namely the sixth to seventh centuries A.D., the prototype of the Barlaam and Josaphat legend was translated from the Pehlevi version into Syriac. Certain cultural and historical evidence has led another scholar to the view that the first Christian recension of *Balavariani* was created during the seventh century in Syriac at the Nestorian capital of India, on the basis of a Pehlevi version of the life story of Buddha.[2]

It is further assumed that the *Balavariani* was at some stage translated from the Pehlevi into Arabic. The appearance of this translation is ascribed to the period of the first 'Abbasid caliphs, namely the eighth and ninth centuries A.D., when the country's cultural efflorescence was accompanied by the revival of literature in Arabic, both translations and original works. Confirma-

---

[1] See I. Yu. Krachkovsky's introduction to *Povest' o Varlaame pustynnike i Iosafe tsareviche indiiskom* ('Story of Varlaam the hermit and Iosaf the Indian prince'), translated from the Arabic by Baron V. R. Rosen, Moscow, 1947, pp. 7-8.

[2] This theory was once advanced by the late Professor K. S. Kekelidze: see his essay 'Balavaris romani k'ristianul mdserlobashi' ('The Balavar romance in Christian literature'), reprinted in *Etiudebi dzveli k'art'uli literaturis istoriidan* ('Studies in the history of Ancient Georgian literature'), vol. VI, Tbilisi, 1960, pp. 44-46.

INTRODUCTION

tion of this is provided by a writer of the second half of the tenth century, Abu'l-Faraj al-Nadim by name, author of a bibliographical treatise called *Kitab al-Fihrist*, which gives a list of works of Indian literary origin, naming among them a 'Book about Bilauhar and Būdasaf', and a separate and distinct 'Book of Būdasaf by himself'. No early manuscripts of these two works, as translated from Pehlevi into Arabic, have yet come to light. The only version which has come down to us is the *Book of Bilauhar and Būdasaf*, published for the first time in lithographed form at Bombay in 1889. It is only by means of this edition, as well as by a defective Muslim Arabic text published earlier by F. Hommel, that we can arrive at any conclusions relating to the early Arabic version of *Balavariani* when this work still bore a close relationship to its original source. There has also been preserved in Arabic another version of the Barlaam romance, which, as H. Zotenberg demonstrated in 1886, is a translation of the Greek recension of the *Life*, dating from a comparatively late period and made in an Arabic-speaking Christian environment.

None of the earliest surviving manuscript copies of the Greek 'Life of Barlaam and Ioasaph' is older than the eleventh century. At least 140 other copies dating from later centuries have also been preserved. A Latin version, translated from the Greek in 1048, has reached us in a manuscript of the fourteenth century. The books about Barlaam and Josaphat in other European languages all derive without exception from either the Greek or the Latin, or are the product of translations made from these two languages. The Armenian 'Life of Barlaam and Ioasaph', the oldest copy of which dates from the year 1322, was also translated from the Greek.

2. MAIN STAGES IN THE CRITICAL STUDY OF THE STORY OF BARLAAM AND IOASAPH. THE GEORGIAN 'BALAVARIANI'.

Since 1886, when the French scholar Zotenberg initiated the critical study of the Greek 'Story of Barlaam and Ioasaph', many specialists have turned their attention towards Georgian literature. Their interest was attracted in the first instance by the fact that the headings of certain Greek manuscripts describe the book as having been translated from the Georgian language into

Greek, with the further indication that the work of translation was done by Euthymius the Georgian (Iberian). Although Zotenberg and other Western European scholars of the last century did not consider this piece of information to be reliable, none the less it played a useful part in arousing interest in Georgian mediaeval literature and particularly in stimulating a search for Georgian manuscripts of *Balavariani*.

A whole group of Russian Orientalists, headed by the well-known Arabic scholar V. R. Rosen, joined in the study of the *Balavariani* problem. V. R. Rosen forthwith invited his pupil N. Y. Marr to participate in these scholarly researches. Marr endorsed his teacher's hypothesis, who considered it possible that the Greek version was translated from an Old Georgian text and postulated in addition that the Georgian version of *Balavariani* had its roots in the Syriac, and embarked with great zeal on the search for *Balavariani* manuscripts. His efforts were soon crowned with success: he discovered one of these manuscripts and published excerpts from it in 1889, under the title 'The Wisdom of Balavar, a Georgian version of the Edifying Story of Barlaam and Ioasaph'. It is true that Rosen's theory was not entirely confirmed by the publication of this, nor was the Georgian text generally accepted as the prototype of the Greek version; from another standpoint, however, as Rosen pointed out, it meant that 'the possibility that this famous story penetrated into Georgian literature via the Syriac can scarcely be definitely ruled out at this stage'.[1]

Soon after N. Y. Marr's discovery of a Georgian manuscript copy of *Balavariani*, the heading of which gives the story's title as 'The Wisdom of Balavar', other manuscripts also came to light. On the basis of these, the historian E. T'aqaishvili published the first edition of *The Wisdom of Balavar* as a separate book in 1895. To make the romance more widely available in scholarly circles, it was translated into Russian by I. A. Javakhishvili and published in 1899.

With the publication of these Russian and Georgian materials,

---

[1] V. R(osen): Review of N. Y. Marr's edition of the 'Life of Peter the Iberian', *Zapiski Vostochnago Otdeleniya*, etc., St Petersburg, tom X, fasc. 1-4, p. 201. Baron Rosen considered that the Syriac origins of the 'Life of Peter the Iberian' confirmed his previously expressed view that *The Wisdom of Balavar* likewise derived from the Syriac. This opinion, incidentally, was also received favourably by Fr. Hommel in 1890.

the study of *Balavariani* gradually took on greater depth and breadth. Unremitting efforts were made to discover new texts. Both in Georgia and abroad, new manuscripts in the Georgian language were found, deriving from an even earlier period than those already known. Among the copies discovered within Georgia, the very earliest, which has survived only in fragmentary form, can be ascribed on palaeographic grounds to the twelfth or thirteenth centuries. This variant has been twice published, first by A. Khakhanov, and then by Mose Janashvili. Complete texts of *The Wisdom of Balavar*, dating from the sixteenth to the eighteenth centuries, were also found. On the basis of these manuscripts, the second edition of *The Wisdom of Balavar* was prepared and published by Ilia Abuladze in 1937.

Copies of *Balavariani* were also discovered beyond the borders of Georgia, namely in the collection of Georgian manuscripts at Jerusalem. One of these, No. 36, attributed to the thirteenth or fourteenth centuries, was described by Nicholas Marr in 1902. Another copy of *Balavariani*, No. 140, consisting of two portions, was discovered by Robert Blake and described briefly in 1925-6 together with the manuscript discovered earlier, Jer. 36.

These Jerusalem copies became fully accessible only in 1956, and then, in view of their great importance, were made the basis for a new, third edition of the work in the Georgian language, under the editorship of Ilia Abuladze. (It is on this edition that the translation in this present volume is based.)

Now what is the special importance of the Jerusalem manuscripts of *Balavariani*?

Up to 1956, no text of the *Wisdom of Balavar* earlier than the sixteenth or seventeenth century was available. The Jerusalem manuscript No. 36 gave scholars their first opportunity to avail themselves of an earlier, complete text of the shorter recension of *The Wisdom of Balavar*, dating from the thirteenth to fourteenth centuries. This text gives better readings of specific passages, and furthermore contains one passage, highly remarkable from a theological viewpoint, which has been omitted from all other copies altogether.

Even greater significance attaches to the second Jerusalem manuscript of *Balavariani*, Jer. 140. Its primary importance consists in the fact that it represents a completely separate redaction which surpasses *The Wisdom of Balavar* both in length (it is two and a half times as long as the short *Wisdom of Balavar*), in antiquity (it was copied in the second half of the eleventh century), and, as we shall see later on, in the early date of its composition.

3. THE TWO OLDEST REDACTIONS OF THE ROMANCE —THE GEORGIAN AND THE GREEK. THE ORIGINS OF THE GEORGIAN 'BALAVARIANI'.

Since scholarly study of *Balavariani* began, and especially since the discovery of its Georgian version, a vital task has been to elucidate the mutual relationship between the two most ancient Christian versions—the Greek *Life of Barlaam and Ioasaph* and the Georgian *Wisdom of Balavar*. N. Y. Marr to begin with, and subsequently such well-informed scholars and specialists in Georgian language and literature as Father Paul Peeters, R. L. Wolff and others, notwithstanding the fact that the Georgian *Wisdom of Balavar* and the Greek *Life of Barlaam and Ioasaph* do not fully correspond textually with one another, recognized none the less that the Georgian work is the source of the Greek version, and accepted as reliable the statement given in the headings to certain Greek manuscripts, to the effect that Euthymius the Iberian had rendered the 'Balavar' story from Georgian into Greek.

When they came to elucidate the characteristic features of the Georgian *Balavariani* and compare it with the Greek, scholars also touched on the question of the origins of the Georgian version itself. Parting company with N. Y. Marr's earlier conclusions, namely that traces of Syriac influence in the *Wisdom of Balavar* proved that the Georgian version derived from the Syriac, Father Peeters observed that the *Wisdom of Balavar* contained distinct traces of Arabic language influence, and considered that the Georgian version indubitably stemmed from the Arabic.[1] This latter view was also supported by Professor Robert Lee Wolff of Harvard University.

[1] P. Peeters, 'La première traduction latine de "Barlaam et Joasaph" et son original grec' in *Analecta Bollandiana*, XLIX, 1931, pp. 303-7. It is worth noting that Marr himself had later admitted that the Syriac elements which he had detected in the *Wisdom of Balavar* might be accounted for in terms of Arabic language influence. (See Marr, 'Agiograficheskie materialy, *etc.*', pt. 2, in *Zapiski Vostochnago Otdeleniya*, St Petersburg, tom. XIII, 1901, pp. 101-2.) Still later, in a book written in 1928 but published only after his death, Marr wrote: 'It is a fact that it (i.e. *The Wisdom of Balavar*) is translated from the Arabic'. (N. Y. Marr, *Gruzinsky yazyk*, Tskhinvali, 1949, p. 26.)

INTRODUCTION

Such then were the opinions about the character and significance of the Georgian *Wisdom of Balavar* which circulated in scholarly circles right up to the 1950s. At that point, the opinions we have cited began to be questioned and even sharply criticized—especially the identification of Euthymius the Iberian as author of the Greek version—and this, naturally enough, provoked an equally determined defence of this latter view by those who held it.

In 1953 the eminent Byzantine scholar, Professor Franz Dölger, published a book[1] in which he attacked these assumptions and historical data according to which the Greek version of the Barlaam Romance stems from the Georgian and was translated or else adapted in metaphrastic form by Euthymius the Georgian (Iberian), affirming that this Greek version in the form in which we possess it belongs to the pen of Saint John Damascene (c. 676-749?), as indicated, in his view, by the preambles of certain manuscripts of the Greek version.

Professor Franz Dölger's assertions, and his unwarranted doubt about the genuineness of the statement by St George the Athonite, biographer of Euthymius the Iberian, to the effect that Euthymius translated 'Balavar' from Georgian into Greek, did not win acceptance in scholarly circles. Several specialists, among them F. Halkin, M. Tarkhnishvili, Shalva Nutsubidze and D. M. Lang, exposed the author's contradictory and tendentious mode of argument, and his lack of knowledge about the problems of Georgian language and literature, and criticized his mistaken conception of Georgian literature, which can be traced back to Zotenberg. One or two leading scholars, however, notably Professor Henri Grégoire and Professor Gérard Garitte, upheld Dölger's conclusions, or at least certain of them.

In the course of this controversy with Professor Dölger, there was also formulated one entirely novel and individual conception of the origins of the Georgian version of *Balavariani*, which failed to attract much support among scholars.[2] We refer to the theory of Professor Shalva Nutsubidze, a member of the

---

[1] Franz Dölger, *Der griechische Barlaam-Roman ein Werk des H. Johannes von Damaskos*, Ettal, 1953.

[2] See P. Devos, 'Les origines du "Barlaam et Joasaph" grec. À propos de la thèse nouvelle de M. Nucubidze', in *Analecta Bollandiana*, tom. LXXV, fasc. 1-2, Bruxelles, 1957, pp. 83-104.

Academy of Sciences of the Georgian S.S.R., according to whom the Georgian romance *Balavariani* (*The Wisdom of Balavar*) is a literary monument of the seventh century A.D. — an original composition written, like the Georgian *Limonarion* or 'Spiritual Paradise', by the Byzantine writer John Moschus. According to Nutsubidze's hypothesis, the surname Moschus, in the form 'Meshki', means 'the Georgian', so that John Moschus could have been a Georgian bilingual author writing both in Georgian and in Greek. This view, with a few modifications, has also been espoused by Professor Simon Qaukhchishvili.

4. THE NEW CODEX (JER. 140) OF 'BALAVARIANI' AND THE NEED TO RE-EXAMINE THE PROBLEMS OF THE ROMANCE

In 1956 scholars gained access to the Jerusalem collection of Georgian manuscripts by the medium of microfilms made by an expedition sponsored by the Library of Congress. It was now possible to determine the precise nature of the *Balavariani* codex No. 140, which had already aroused interest when briefly described by Robert P. Blake in 1925-6, both because it consisted of two separate sections, and also because it appeared to be very much longer than the original *Wisdom of Balavar*. The present writer was the first person in Georgia to uncover the new text of *Balavariani* among the microfilms of the Jerusalem collection. During the editing of this extremely interesting text, which turned out to be a completely new redaction, photographic and manuscript copies of the work were made available also to other interested specialists in Old Georgian literature. The work was studied with lively energy, and a number of scholarly studies devoted to the new text were published in Georgia. In Western Europe, David Marshall Lang, Professor of Caucasian Studies at the University of London, discovered this text among the Jerusalem microfilms quite independently of us, and was the first to investigate and analyze it. The late Father Michael Tarkhnishvili also devoted a separate article to the new version and to publications connected with it.

With the appearance of this new, full-length text of *Balavariani*, it naturally became a matter of urgent importance to clear up the relationship between the shorter *Wisdom of Balavar* and the new redaction. This was bound to lead to

INTRODUCTION

reappraisal of the relationship of the Georgian *Balavariani* romance to the Greek version as well as to the Arabic, a connection which had already been established by reference to the short *Wisdom of Balavar*.

As might have been anticipated, such specialists as Professor Shalva Nutsubidze, who looked on the shorter *Wisdom of Balavar* as an authentic original record of an oral narrative by an Indian story teller, failed to attribute any great value to the newly discovered *Balavariani* text. Those scholars, on the other hand, to whom comparative analysis showed that the *Wisdom of Balavar* is an abridgement of the newly discovered text, set out afresh to tackle the main questions concerning the links between the longer *Balavariani* text and the other main Christian versions of the story, with particular reference to the Greek one, as well as the problem of the origins of the longer Georgian *Balavariani* itself.

One of the first to discuss the new Georgian redaction of *Balavariani* was the late Professor Korneli Kekelidze, an outstanding historian of Georgian literature and a member of the Academy of Sciences of the Georgian S.S.R. In his article 'The Balavar romance in Christian literature', written in 1956,[1] he examines first of all one of the main questions, namely: 'When and in what language was the Christian version of the Barlaam and Ioasaph romance first elaborated, and how did it take on that particular form which is designated today as the Greek redaction?'

In Professor Kekelidze's opinion, the first Christian version was composed in the Syriac tongue. This might well have occurred at the period when the Indian Metropolitan see of the Eastern Nestorian Church in company with the Persian national Metropolitan sees entered into a struggle with the Seleucia-Ctesiphon Catholicosate to secure independence for their own Church. In the mid-seventh century, as is well known, there was a proposal to create a new Catholicosate which, in order to justify its pretensions to rank as an independent Church, felt the need for a document which would establish that this Church possessed an Apostle of its own. It was desirable first and fore-

[1] Reprinted in K. S. Kekelidze, *Etiudebi dzveli k'art'uli literaturis istoriidan* ('Studies in the history of Ancient Georgian literature'), vol. VI, Tbilisi, 1960, pp. 41-71.

most to establish this by suitable literary evidence. 'To achieve this purpose,' K. S. Kekelidze wrote, 'it was necessary first of all to suppress the legend of the implanting of Christianity in India by the Apostle Thomas, the enlightener of the Syrians.' As a substitute for this tradition, a romance about St Barlaam was composed in the middle of the seventh century in the Syriac language, based on the Pehlevi redaction of the Life of Buddha, its underlying purpose, as would appear from the Georgian redactions, being 'to prove that the enlightener of India was not the Apostle Thomas, but the Indian prince Ioasaph and his teacher Barlaam'. When this first Christian recension of the *Story of Barlaam and Ioasaph* had played its role, it was consigned to oblivion and lost. Today, science has at its disposal two Christian adaptations of it only—the Georgian and the Greek.

In Professor Kekelidze's essay, the following questions are also discussed: (a) What is the connection between the two Georgian redactions? (b) What is the link between the newly discovered Georgian redaction and the non-Christian Arabic version? (c) What is the relationship between the shorter Georgian text of *Balavariani* and the Greek version? (d) What connection is there between the extended Georgian text of *Balavariani* and the Greek romance?

Dealing with the connection between the two Georgian redactions, Professor Kekelidze points out that the *Balavariani* story as previously known, also called *The Wisdom of Balavar*, is an abbreviated text, whereas the newly discovered redaction is an extended, unabridged one. The abridged text 'is in the main free from those lengthy and abstract dissertations on Christian morality and religious dogma with which the full-length redaction abounds'. A few of the abstract dissertations are given in a brief and condensed form. Both versions coincide in their general content, but in places the same idea is conveyed in different words, or is expressed by the same words rearranged in a different order. 'As a result of comparing both redactions, it can be established that a genetic link exists between them. We have every reason to assume Redaction A (i.e. the short one) to be an abridgement of Redaction B (i.e. the long one), prepared for certain specific purposes.' This work of abridgement, in Kekelidze's view, was undertaken in order to adapt the story for use by the Church as a piece of devotional literature.

INTRODUCTION

To the question concerning the link between the full-length Georgian *Balavariani* and the surviving Arabic non-Christian version, Professor Kekelidze gives the following answer: Generally speaking, the Georgian full-length redaction 'takes its origin from an Arabic-Christian redaction, based for the most part on a non-Christian Arabic version deriving from the Pehlevi Life of Buddha'. At the same time, 'the second part of the story, namely the collapse of Thedma's plot (the Arabic gives his name as al-Bahwan), and the conversion of King Abenes to Christianity, finds no equivalent in the Arabic story. The author of the Christian version, evidently motivated by his different ideological outlook and by his desire to give the story a Christian flavour, altered the ending of the Arabic version and adapted it in his own individual manner'. In the first part of the Georgian *Balavariani*, according to Kekelidze, the author 'faithfully follows the Arabic text, though in this section the Arabic redaction is more diffuse. The Christian writer did his best to select his subject matter in a way consistent with his Christian outlook, and with this in view, he made many omissions. The general narrative framework, and its layout and arrangement, correspond completely in both Georgian and Arabic versions. As for the dogmatic and ethical aspect, and the philosophical reasonings and dissertations generally, all this could obviously not be taken wholesale from the Arabic and incorporated in its entirety in a Christian story without undergoing some modification in the process.'

Leaving aside the work's actual contents, K. S. Kekelidze considered that the derivation of the longer Georgian version from the Arabic was attested by certain traces of Arabic influence in vocabulary and syntax, as had already been pointed out in the short redaction by N. Y. Marr. The dependence of the Georgian version on the Arabic, he further observed, is revealed by analysis of names of characters and places occurring in the narrative, for instance *Balahvar*, coming from Arabic *Bilawhar*; *Iodasaph*, from Arabic *Būdasaf*; the Georgian and Arabic *Rakhis* as contrasted with the Greek form *Araches*; the Georgian and Arabic place name *Sarandib* (i.e. Ceylon), as contrasted with the Greek *Senaar*; and the Georgian *Sholait* (as the name of King Abenes's capital), coming from the Arabic form *Shawilabat*.

As mentioned above, Professor Kekelidze considered that the

longer redaction of *Balavariani* stems from a so far undiscovered Christian Arabic version of the romance which, in his opinion, could not have originated earlier than the ninth century, seeing that the work, 'having been translated from Pehlevi into Arabic in the second half of the eighth century, could not have been adapted into a Christian romance prior to the ninth century'. This factor in turn helps to determine the date of composition of the full-length Georgian *Balavariani*, which Kekelidze regarded as a translation made by the Georgian colony in Palestine from a Christian Arabic version at the turn of the ninth to tenth centuries. The same scholar ascribes the short redaction to the end of the tenth century.

After comparing the Georgian redactions of *Balavariani* with the Greek version, which, like the Georgian full-length version, retains Arabic elements in its subject matter, as well as accurately reproducing the conclusion of the Georgian story and showing a resemblance between the forms of the proper names, Professor Kekelidze concluded that the Greek redaction was based on the Georgian redaction of *Balavariani*, and what is more, on the newly-discovered, full-length version.

The same authority concluded that the Greek redaction is far from being a literal translation from the Georgian, but has rather been elaborated after the metaphrastic style of hagiography, with all its characteristic features. From a straightforward translation made by Euthymius the Athonite, it may well have been adapted by the very founder of the metaphrastic school of hagiography, namely Simeon Logothetes, surnamed the Metaphrast, who flourished during the tenth and eleventh centuries.

*   *   *   *

In 1957, when preparing for publication the newly discovered text of the *Balavariani* romance (Jer. 140), along with a parallel edition of the text of the shorter *Wisdom of Balavar* in the previously known abridged version, the present writer naturally had occasion to weigh up certain historical and literary problems connected with these writings. Investigation convinced us too that of these two versions, the one handed down in the unique manuscript dating from the second half of the eleventh century

INTRODUCTION

(Jer. 140) represents the complete and unabridged form of the work, while all other texts, manuscript copies of which date from various times between the twelfth and the eighteenth centuries, contain an abridged version consisting of selections from the original, longer redaction, partly adapted and rewritten. When shortening the text, the mediaeval editor set himself the task of describing more concisely the life story and acts of Balavar and Iodasaph as pioneers in the spreading of Christianity, giving prominence to the action of the tale, and cutting down the abstract and long-winded moral discourses.

The text of the abbreviated version contains linguistic features not met with in Georgian before the end of the eleventh century. This seems in fact to be the period when the abridgement was made. There are one or two passages in *The Wisdom of Balavar* which do not feature at all in the full-length *Balavariani*: certain of these were doubtless introduced by the abridger himself, others possibly introduced from a copy of the full-length version which has not come down to us. Evidence for this is provided by the fact that the one and only text of the full-length version which has survived is a secondary manuscript copy, and not an original autograph or archetype.

The same applies to those portions of the abridged redaction of the story which have undergone some alteration. Such modification may be attributed to the mediaeval editor, though one or two instances may possibly derive from some lost text or variant of *Balavariani* no longer available to us.

*   *   *   *

On gaining access to the full-length Jerusalem redaction of *Balavariani*, the British scholar D. M. Lang, who was the first Western specialist to discover and devote attention to the text of the work, published a new study,[1] in which he stated the Jerusalem text of *Balavariani* to be the original, full-length recension of this work, and *The Wisdom of Balavar* a mere abridgement made for the purpose of including the tale in

---

[1] D. M. Lang, 'The life of the Blessed Iodasaph: a New Oriental Christian Version of the Barlaam and Ioasaph Romance (Jerusalem, Greek Patriarchal Library: Georgian MS 140), in *Bulletin of the School of Oriental and African Studies*, London, XX, 1957, pp. 389-407.

anthologies. In Professor Lang's view, furthermore, the full-length redaction of *Balavariani* is a direct, first-hand adaptation of the *Book of Bilauhar and Būdasaf* and was composed on the basis of the Arabic non-Christian version in the ninth century, this being confirmed by such evidence as the forms of proper names, the sequence in which the fables are arranged, the order of the narrative episodes, and the concordance of sections of the text.

Only a short period of time can have elapsed, Lang thinks, from the appearance of the full-length version of the romance to that of the abridgement, seeing that the shorter text 'contains archaisms characteristic of the ninth century'. In his opinion, the language of the work sometimes recalls that of the Georgian Adish Gospels, copied in A.D. 897. When pointing this out, D. M. Lang cites the observations of Father M. Tarkhnishvili.

Professor Lang also compares the Jerusalem redaction of *Balavariani* with the Greek version, and comes to the conclusion that in the Greek Barlaam romance there is not a single part of the text of any importance (except for the Biblical and Patristic quotations and the *Apology of Aristides*) which is not to be found in the Georgian version. In addition, this scholar notes that the Greek version lacks several fables which occur in the Georgian *Balavariani* romance (e.g. 'The Dogs, the Carrion and the Wayfarer', 'Physician and Patient', and 'The Warrior and his Amorous Wife'), and which derive in their entirety from the Arabic version. In conclusion, Dr Lang affirms that the Georgian *Balavariani* romance in its full-length shape occupies a position midway between the Arabic and the Greek versions, and that the Greek version is entirely dependent on the Georgian.

That distinguished philologist the late Father M. Tarkhnishvili also dealt with the questions bound up with the two Georgian versions of *Balavariani* in an article published by way of commentary on the new pieces of research which we have enumerated.[1] In contrast to our own conviction and to Professor Lang's opinion, namely that *The Wisdom of Balavar* is merely an abridgement of that same full-length version of the romance which was discovered in 1956 among the microfilms of the Jerusalem collection of Georgian manuscripts, Father Tarkhnish-

[1] M. Tarkhnishvili, 'Les deux recensions du "Barlaam" géorgien', in *Le Muséon*, Louvain, tom. LXXI, 1958, pp. 65-86.

vili considered both versions to derive from a common archetype. In his opinion 'there is no direct and immediate link between the longer and the shorter versions of *Balavariani*, and both of them derive from a common source, which is more ancient than the ninth century.'

Both Professor Lang and Father Tarkhnishvili detect the existence of archaic forms in the abridged redaction of *Balavariani*. On this evidence D. M. Lang ascribes the shorter version to the ninth century, whereas M. Tarkhnishvili considered the original appearance of the romance in the Georgian language to antedate the eighth century, that is to say, its original Georgian version may have appeared even before the conquest of Caucasian Iberia by the Arabs.

Father Tarkhnishvili's theory is that the Georgian full-length version, certain passages of which recur in the Greek text, has been adapted to fit in with a lost Arabic text. It was no doubt partly under the influence of this Arabic version that there came into being the dual identity of Balavar which we can trace in the two Georgian redactions.

This theory of Father Tarkhnishvili is based on analysis of the texts of the Georgian *Balavariani* and their archaic features. When attempting to assign a date to literary texts, it is certainly legitimate if direct evidence is lacking to resort to analysis of archaisms in vocabulary and syntax, provided that we know the precise history of their usage and the evolution of their semantic content in a given language. But seeing that these conditions are not fulfilled in regard to Georgian, owing to lack of the requisite historical dictionaries, an element of arbitrariness is bound to creep in when this method is employed.

A more reliable technique for dating literary texts would, in our view, be to pay regard to the occurrence in the relevant writings of words of foreign provenance. Now it is a well-known fact that Georgian literature has since its beginnings incorporated words of Greek, Armenian, Syriac and Middle Persian (Pehlevi) origin. Arabic and New Persian words make their appearance in Georgian literature in their turn, but not before a specific phase in its development: Arabic words came in following the establishment of relations with the Arabs, which could not be reflected in literature prior to the eighth century, and New Persian ones since the time of the formation of the modern Persian language, that is to say, not before the ninth century.[1] It follows from this that if a given Old Georgian text contains words of Arabic or New Persian provenance, let alone syntactical features peculiar to those languages, then such a text cannot belong to a period earlier than the eighth or ninth centuries. When we apply this criterion to the two recensions of *Balavariani*, it becomes clear that neither of them can be ascribed to a period earlier than the eighth or ninth centuries.

This well-tried method of dating literary works has already served as a guide for earlier scholars such as Marr, Javakhishvili, Peeters, Blake and others, and remains applicable to the present day. When determining the date of the shorter *Wisdom of Balavar*, Marr observed that the presence of Persian words such as *susti* ('weak'), *p'lasi* ('a hair shirt'), *changi* ('a lyre'), *pasukhi* ('an answer'), *chabuki* ('a youth', 'a knight') and *laghi* ('bold') seemed to rule out any attempt to assign the work to a period prior to the ninth century. All the above-mentioned words, apart from *changi* and *p'lasi*, are found in the new Jerusalem manuscript of *Balavariani*, which also contains two related terms of New Persian origin, namely *dasturi* ('reliable', 'a trustworthy agent') and *dasturoba* ('trust', 'allegiance'). In addition, however, the new Jerusalem text contains the very common Georgian word *imedi* ('hope'), reproducing precisely the Pehlevi form *imed* (New Persian has *omid*), and the much more characteristic *pahraki* ('sentry', 'minion'), from Parthian/Middle Persian *pahrag* ('sentry', 'watch-post').

M. Tarkhnishvili has disagreed with our deductions on this point, on the ground that the terms *chabuki*, *susti* and *laghi* are encountered in the Georgian Bible, and that the word *pasukhi* is employed in the *Epistles of Arsenius*, translated into Georgian, according to Professor G. Garitte who discovered the Georgian

[1] Dr E. M. Boyce, Professor of Iranian Studies in the University of London, kindly points out that in weighing up the Iranian evidence, it is, of course, important to avoid over-simplification. 'Middle Persian is held to last from c. 300 B.C. — c. A.D. 800. Its chief representative is Pahlavi literature; but the conventions of Pahlavi spelling were largely evolved B.C., and preserved unaltered for several centuries. Since 1904 we have the evidence of the Manichaean texts, written in a clear new orthography from c. A.D. 250; so we now know that many Sasanian words had already developed into the forms known from New Persian.' It is thus important not to operate exclusively from the Pehlevi literary evidence, without taking account of the latest evidence on the chronology of the evolution of Persian.

version, prior to the ninth century. Indeed, Father Tarkhnishvili is right in saying that Iranian words found in ancient copies of the Georgian Bible, dating from the tenth century or earlier, cannot truly be treated as New Persian, because these copies themselves were made from manuscripts of translations completed at an earlier date still. Consequently, despite Marr's view, *chabuki* and *laghi* cannot now be definitely identified as New Persian, and are in this connection to be disregarded. As for *susti* ('weak'), this exists in the form *sust* in Middle and New Persian alike.

The Georgian word *pasukhi* ('an answer') is especially interesting. Dr E. M. Boyce points out that the Old Iranian form is *pati.sakhwan*, giving the Armenian *pataskhan*. Middle Persian has *passōkh*, giving New Persian *pasokh*. The Georgian word seems to reflect this last-mentioned form, which did not enter the Georgian vocabulary before the ninth century.

Father Tarkhnishvili explained two other words, *changi* ('lyre') and *p'lasi* ('hair shirt'), as later interpolations, possibly subsequent to the twelfth century. As for the words *dasturi* ('reliable') and *imedi* ('hope') which we encounter in the full-length *Balavariani* manuscript, Tarkhnishvili says nothing about them at all.

Critical study of the Iranian loan-words in the two redactions of the Georgian Barlaam romance shows them to be a mixed bag. Two seem definitely Middle Persian or Pehlevi, several are common to both Middle and New Persian, but at least two are of New Persian origin. It would be very difficult on this evidence to judge the Georgian version of the Barlaam and Ioasaph romance to be a production of the earliest phase of Georgian literature, the period from the fifth to the eighth century. The data at our disposal lead us rather to consider the full-length redaction of *Balavariani* to be a literary monument of the ninth and tenth centuries, and the condensed version, a product of the end of the eleventh century, if not of an even later time.

5. GENERAL CONCLUSIONS ON THE TWO GEORGIAN REDACTIONS OF THE ROMANCE

With Tarkhnishvili's exception, the scholars just mentioned concur in declaring the full-length *Balavariani* to be the original text of the work, and the shorter one, a condensed version of it.

This conclusion was reached almost simultaneously by K. S. Kekelidze, D. M. Lang and the present writer, working independently of one another. There is general consensus of opinion about the time when the full-length *Balavariani* made its appearance in Georgian. Lang considers that it originated in the ninth century, Kekelidze on the border line between the ninth and tenth centuries, while my own view is that it belongs either to the ninth or the tenth. Scholars' opinions differ only in regard to the appearance of the condensed version. D. M. Lang considers this to date from the ninth century, while affirming that the full-length version of the romance had made its appearance earlier in that same century; K. S. Kekelidze dates it at the end of the tenth century; while I ascribe it to the end of the eleventh century, if not to an even later period. Father Tarkhnishvili, as was pointed out, held an altogether different view of the matter.

What are the sources of the full-length redaction of *Balavariani*? On this point also, the scholars concerned do not disagree to any great extent. K. S. Kekelidze and D. M. Lang give a straightforward answer. The latter considers that the longer version of *Balavariani* represents an original Christian adaptation in the Georgian language of the Arabic *Book of Bilauhar and Būdasaf*. Professor Kekelidze views it as a translation from a still undiscovered Christian Arabic recension. Dr Lang's theory appears to be the correct one. Had an earlier Christian version of the romance existed in the Arabic tongue, then one feels that the Arabic-speaking Christians would not have needed later on to translate the story from the Greek version, especially as this latter is markedly inferior from the literary viewpoint even to the Arabic non-Christian version (from which the Christian version itself is presumed to derive) and also to the Georgian full-length redaction, which in one fashion or another proceeds from an Arabic source.

6. NEW DATA ATTESTING THE LINKS BETWEEN THE GEORGIAN 'BALAVARIANI', AND THE GREEK AND ARABIC VERSIONS OF THE ROMANCE

The general opinions just outlined concerning the derivation of the full-length version of *Balavariani* from the Arabic version, and the fact that the Georgian redaction is the source of the

INTRODUCTION

Greek one, can now be confirmed by one or two new additional factors.

In the first place, we shall discuss the manner in which the name of the Indian king Abenes, Iodasaph's father, is transformed in its transition from the Arabic version into the Georgian, and then from the Georgian into the Greek.

In manuscripts of the shorter redaction of *Balavariani* and that of the full-length redaction, the name *Abenes* occurs also in the various forms *Hebenas*, *Abenese*, or *Iabenes*. Not long ago, there was discovered an Old Georgian hymn dedicated to Iodasaph which, according to Ts. Jghamaia, who edited it for publication, was composed prior to another, well-known hymn to St Iodasaph written by St George the Athonite (1009-65).[1] In this newly discovered hymn, an English translation of which is given later in the present volume, the Indian king bears the name *Abeneser*. Analysis of all the various forms of the name encountered in Georgian manuscripts of the work shows that *Abeneser* is certainly the original and authentic spelling, probably with an initial 'H': *Habeneser*. Now the final syllable of this name—the element *-ser*—is an echo of the ending of the Arabic form of the Indian king's name—*Janaisar*. The three preceding consonants in the name, 'H', 'b' and 'n', are in fact nothing but the Arabic 'J', 'n' and 'i' in disguise. As is well known, these letters are distinguished from one another in Arabic by the insertion of one or more dots above or below the line. The letters in question have either been wrongly read because of the inability of the scribe or the translator to make out the diacritical marks in the Arabic, or are the result of an independent attempt to decipher a text written without any diacritical marks at all.

When we come to compare the Georgian transcription of the name *Habeneser* with the Greek *Abenner*, we find ourselves more convinced than ever of the dependence of the Greek version on the Georgian *Balavariani*.

The fact that the Georgian version of *Balavariani* stems in its turn from the Arabic is confirmed by an important indication of a different character, namely the presence in the Georgian

[1] Ts. Jghamaia, 'Iodasap'is sagaloblis akhali varianti' ('A new variant of the hymn to Iodasaph'), in *Khelnadsert'a institutis moambe* ('Bulletin of the Institute of Manuscripts'), Tbilisi, III, 1961, pp. 33-57.

37

text of a syntactical feature especially characteristic of Arabic.

It is a known fact that in Arabic, the conjunction *wa* ('and'— in Georgian, *da*) is employed in compound sentences not only for joining together co-ordinate clauses of equal rank, but also for joining subordinate temporal clauses to the main sentence. In such instances, the contemporary Georgian language normally has recourse to the words *mashin* ('then'), *mashin rotsa* ('at the time when') or *rodesats* ('when').

Now it is noteworthy that this Arabic syntactical peculiarity which we have noted can be detected in the Georgian *Balavariani*, but only in the full-length version. Consider for instance the following passage in Ilia Abuladze's edition of 1957, p. 81, lines 20-24. Translated literally, the text reads: 'Iodasaph said: "How can the poorest of your companions be richer than I *and* you spoke of their extreme poverty? Or how should I become miserly when my treasures are multiplied, *and* I am lavish in giving today?"'

In other words: 'Iodasaph said: "How comes it that the poorest of your companions is richer than I, after what you have been saying about their extreme poverty? How is it that I shall become miserly when my treasures are multiplied, whereas today I am lavish in giving?"'

A similar illustration of the recurrence of this Arabic grammatical peculiarity in the Georgian text is provided on page 139 of Abuladze's edition, lines 26-38.

7. THE PLACE OF 'BALAVARIANI' IN WORLD LITERATURE

Study of the full-length Georgian redaction of *Balavariani* shows that the Greek Barlaam romance has its roots in this Georgian text, and that the Georgian is the *keimenon*, that is, the original, unembellished version, from which the Greek metaphrastic, i.e. stylized and ornate, adaptation derives. Once this has been demonstrated—and the facts are now established beyond doubt —it must be asked who is to be acknowledged as the author of the Greek version if not Euthymius the Georgian (Iberian), as stated in the headings of certain Greek manuscripts of the Life of Barlaam? The author of the Barlaam romance indisputably had a first-rate command of both Georgian and Greek. Now that a new Georgian redaction of *Balavariani* has been found, having

INTRODUCTION

many points of contact with the Greek text, the voice of Euthymius the Iberian's biographer, George the Athonite, has an especially convincing ring today when he declares that 'Father Euthymius rendered from Georgian into Greek Balahvari and Abukura and a number of other works'.[1]

The fact that out of the Georgian version of *Balavariani* there originated the Greek version, which gave rise in turn to the further diffusion of this highly remarkable mediaeval romance among many peoples of the West and the East, speaks eloquently of the value of Georgian literature's contribution to the treasury of world literature.

This contribution is not an accidental one. From the fifth century of our era, the Georgian people succeeded in establishing and maintaining a vigorous connection with the outside world, and in keeping up close cultural relationships with the Christian Occident and Orient. These links, which arose out of common ideological convictions, helped to bring the cultures of the various Christian nations closer together and enabled them to borrow items of spiritual value from one another. From an early period, the Georgians developed literary relations with the Syrians, the Armenians, the Greeks, the Arabs and other nations. Research into the character and extent of these cultural and literary relationships shows that wherever Georgian cultural centres grew up and enjoyed favourable conditions for development, they always played an active role in establishing and strengthening links with other nations possessing a written literature. These links were not of a one-sided nature, but were mutual in character.

After making contact with peoples writing in the Arabic tongue, members of the Georgian communities in Jerusalem and its environs took the opportunity to translate into Georgian some remarkable works of Christian literature written in Arabic, both in the way of translations and original writings. These Georgian translations from Arabic cover various branches of literature. Among them are found hagiographical, ascetic, exegetical and other works. One of the hagiographical texts is even translated in rhymed form. This is the second of the two works which, according to St George the Athonite, were trans-

[1] D. M. Lang, *Lives and Legends of the Georgian Saints*, London, Allen & Unwin, New York, Macmillan, 1956, p. 155.

lated from Georgian into Greek by Euthymius the Georgian, the other being *Balavariani*. The work in question, which George the Athonite refers to as 'Abukura', is in reality known as 'The Martyrdom of Saint Michael, who dwelt in the Lavra of our holy Father Saba'.[1]

Particularly extensive and fruitful were the relations established with the Greek literary world in the time of the Byzantine Empire. There remained scarcely a single noteworthy work of any creative originality which was not absorbed into Georgian literature. The Georgians kept a constant watch on the evolution of literatures of the most highly developed Christian nations, and did not leave a single important literary event without making reference to it at the time.

In the case of *Balavariani*, Old Georgian literature did not lag behind other Oriental Christian communities in adapting and translating this intensely interesting literary production. There is no doubt that Georgian writers found the romance attractive not only for its subject matter, but also for its artistic form.

It has already been pointed out that a great artistic role was played by the fables, which serve to illustrate with inimitable vividness certain of Barlaam's involved moral and dogmatic propositions. The full-length Georgian redaction of *Balavariani* even exceeds the Greek Barlaam romance in the number of its fables, which provides evidence of its high artistic merit.

The spiritual life and practical activity of the main and secondary heroes of the romance are portrayed in the full-length redaction of the Georgian *Balavariani* story with exceptional skill and power. In this romance, there are none of the miraculous incidents, 'marvels' or 'signs' which religious fancy tends to produce, a factor which distinguishes the Georgian story from the Greek version, and even to some extent from the shortened Georgian *Wisdom of Balavar*. It may be worth recalling the apt description of the Georgian Barlaam romance as a work of literary art given by Academician N. Y. Marr, who wrote:

'The magic charm of the work lies in the artistic realism of the

[1] K. S. Kekelidze, 'Romani "Abukura" da misi ori redak'tsia dzvel k'art'ul mdserlobashi' ('The Abukura Romance and its two versions in Old Georgian literature'), in *Etiudebi dzveli k'art'uli literaturis istoriidan* ('Studies in the history of Ancient Georgian literature'), vol. VI, Tbilisi, 1960, pp. 18-40.

INTRODUCTION

narrative. This realism, so typical of the most ancient Christian version — namely the Georgian one — survives in artistic form and preserves its force even beneath the inartistic scholastic overlay superimposed in the Greek version. This artistic realism is characteristic of all redactions, both Christian and Muslim, in proportion to the extent that their archaic features have not been obscured, and I would repeat that it emerges with especial clarity in the Georgian version . . . Here the story's heroes are so much alive, their tale is told in such a simple and convincing manner, that the reader, even a contemporary one, lives through their life-story with them.'[1]

Marr wrote this when he had access only to the condensed redaction of *Balavariani,* or *The Wisdom of Balavar.* This description can be applied in its entirety and with even greater aptness to the full-length version as well, for in comparison with the short text, the latter's artistic merits are even more clear and convincing.

In the Greek Barlaam Romance, as contrasted with the Georgian *Balavariani,* the reader's attention is distracted by the plethora of quotations from the Scriptures and from ecclesiastical writers, especially from the works of St John Damascene. Every thesis, every statement of a theological or dogmatic character, is accompanied by extracts or quotations from the Bible and other religious and philosophical sources. Such extracts are so copious throughout the Greek Romance that the fables which are used to illustrate it lose a large part of their artistic and illustrative character, and are drowned in endless abstract dissertations.

Such are the main and most conspicuous differences between the Georgian and Greek versions of *Balavariani.* From the point of view of literary artistry, the Greek version is inferior to the Georgian. In the Greek text, the simplicity of exposition and consummate artistry characteristic of the Georgian full-length redaction are sacrificed to verbosity and a mass of quotations from the Bible and theological books, as is characteristic of metaphrastic versions of lives of Christian saints.

I. V. ABULADZE

Institute of Manuscripts
3 Rustaveli Avenue, Tbilisi, Georgian S.S.R.

---

[1] N. Y. Marr, 'Agiograficheskie materialy, *etc.*', pt. 2, in *Zapiski Vostochnago Otdeleniya,* St Petersburg, tom. XIII, 1901, pp. 94-95.

A HYMN TO THE BLESSED IODASAPH

The Georgian text of the following hymn dates back to the ninth or the tenth century. It is taken from Manuscript No. 42 of the Georgian collection in the Greek Patriarchal Library in Jerusalem, which was copied not later than A.D. 1065.[1]

May 19. *Commemoration of the Noble and Meritorious Saint Iodasaph, King of the Indians*

Intercede with Christ our God before whom you stand, O God-enlightened worthy monarch, O Iodasaph illustrious in merit, that He may inspire us worthily to adorn your holy anniversary and fashion for you a diadem of praise to the utmost of our powers.

Most exalted, blessed one, wisdom was granted to you from heaven, and you were made worthy of apostolic grace; for you released the race of the Indians by God's power from their benighted devil-worship and brought them into the service of the God of all mankind, O blessed one.

Although this tongue in its impotence is incapable of portraying the multitude of your feats of piety, whereby you dedicated yourself from your youth to the love of God our Saviour who granted you the crown of holiness, yet it must offer at least some trifling meed of tribute from these unworthy lips in unison with the choir.

By the invincible power of God you put to shame, O worthy one, enemies both visible and invisible and trampled their cohorts entirely under foot. For you had as your guide the life-giving and invincible might of the Cross and thereby put hideous Belial to flight.

[1] Our translation of the Georgian text of the hymn has been made from the edition by Ts. Jghamaia, in *Khelnadsert'a institutis moambe* ('Bulletin of the Institute of Manuscripts'), Tbilisi, III, 1961, pp. 45-57.

You are a candle shining bright upon a lofty candlestick, nor could the sinister frenzy of the loathsome idolaters hide you, O worthy one! Rather did you shine forth the more brightly by the light of the Holy Trinity, and you dispelled the murk and lit up the land.

You have been exalted, O righteous one, like a planet brilliant in virtues, and soared aloft on the wings of the spirit and rose above the level of mortal nature; for you offered up countless fruit as a sacrifice to God in sweet savour, and you extirpated the temples of the idols and established churches instead.

From the broad way which leads to perdition you departed afar, O blessed one, and you clung fast to the narrow road which leads to salvation. Therefore Christ our God exalted you with glory everlasting, set upon you the imperishable crown, and assigned you a place among the immortal souls. Therefore the Church today adorns your festival with brilliant panoply and rejoices with its children; for the children of the barren are multiplied and the prolific womb is exhausted.

You were filled with divine wisdom, O blessed one, and did valiantly withstand that fearsome king, your father Abeneser,[1] and you quelled his strength by the unconquerable power of God which abode in you, O blessed one. Thus you became a parent to your own father, O God-clad one, and enlightened him by divine wisdom, and made him worthy to be born again by baptism of water and the Holy Ghost, and brought him renewed into God's presence like a sweet-scented offering on to the heavenly altar.

When your God-clad and blessed teacher Balahvar was informed by the Holy Spirit of the problems which beset you, O blessed one, he cast out all human fear and dread of death, and like a valiant knight of Christ he came and filled you with spiritual wisdom, and exposed clearly to you the vanity and transitory nature of this world. And your heart and mind were illumined, O blessed one; and he filled you with spiritual joy.

You are united with the ranks of the apostles, O worthy one, divinely exalted king: for you also strove as they did, preached

---

[1] As pointed out by Professor Abuladze in his Introduction, this form of the king's name is important, since it provides a link between the Arabic form, *Janaisar*, and the Greek, *Abenner*. In the Georgian *Balavariani* manuscripts, a more usual form is *Abenes*, this being a later, shortened variant.

the gospel of salvation, and brought beneath the authority of our God countless peoples who were held captive by the foe. You became a son of the Church by baptism and brilliantly irradiated the assembly of the Christians by the light of God, and darkened the eyes of the evil and infernal apostates; and you preached aloud the single essence of the Trinity, being one God and indivisible.

O come, ye faithful, and sing an anthem to him!

The Lord of the planets, Lucifer, who first established his throne upon the clouds and vied with God the Creator of all— he now was trampled underfoot by Iodasaph with God's aid, like some humble sparrow, together with all his host.

Who can enumerate the feats which you undertook for the sake of Christ our God, O valiant warrior, blessed one of illustrious deeds, or utter them aloud? For they excel the nature of mortals! But we shall not hold back from praising them to the extent of our powers.

The evil foe of mankind, ever eager for our destruction, strove to strip from you the mantle of purity, and incited the king to tempt you by means of women's wiles. But you, like some incorporeal being, crushed his power by your own weak flesh.

The commemoration of the pious Iodasaph resembles a white rose imparting fragrance to the faithful throng and perfuming all who approach to adorn his festival day brilliantly fair and worthy of our anthems.

Rejoice, O blessed one, elect of God, supreme among all kings, most worthy Iodasaph, pride of the Christians and fair ornament of the Churches.

With the bright-toned organ we adorn with praise that worthy treasure of wisdom, that wondrous man, the God-clad Iodasaph, pride and bastion of Christian folk.

Rejoice then, God-clad one, together with the holy King David, called the father of God; for you followed on his tracks without wavering and were glorified with him by Christ, O righteous one, for all eternity.

For you have earned the grace of the apostles, the martyrs and the just, O worthy one, and now you are united with that incorporeal throng and radiantly lit up by the beacon of the Trinity.

You rejected the glory of kingship, O blessed one, and put on the sweet yoke of monastic life; and you crucified yourself unto the world for God's sake, and the world was crucified unto you, according to the words of the Apostle.[1]

Your deeds excel the nature of mortal man, O blessed king; for like some disembodied being you withstood the invisible foe in those impassable desert places.

You made haste like a deer towards the well-spring and wandered from place to place, O blessed one, seeking for your good teacher Balahvar; and when you had found him, you glorified God.

In place of transitory kingship, O blessed one, you chose the glory which is permanent and unending, and you rejoice in unspeakable and eternal happiness.

Golden rivers flowed from your body, O God-clad one, wherewith you watered the parched earth, fertilized its furrows, and made the young grass of God's service to sprout by the stream of your tears.

You were filled with the Holy Ghost and strongly opposed the multitude of the foe; and you put to naught all their devices by the power of God and cut out their tongues with the sword of the spirit, O wise one.

You bravely denounced the godlessness of your opponents, declaring: 'Those idols which you serve are loathsome devils and deceivers of men. How is it that you are so devoid of understanding?'

You kindled a divine spark within your father's heart, and the darkness of his mind's eyes was illumined by the light of the knowledge of God, and the soul-destroying murk was dissipated.

O Trinity all in One, God by nature inaccessible, it was by Thy help that Thy blessed and virtuous servant, the worthy Iodasaph, was given strength to trample on the power of the foe.

That promise which Thou didst make by those lips that lie not to those that place their hope in Thee, O Christ our God, Thou hast performed towards those who have fearlessly confessed Thy divine nature before the tyrant's face.

Immortal king, God the Creator of all, look down upon us with the eye of mercy as we celebrate the commemoration of Iodasaph the Christian hero.

---

[1] Galatians, vi.14: 'But God forbid that I should glory, save in the cross of Our Lord Jesus Christ, by whom the world is crucified unto me, and I unto the world.'

A HYMN TO THE BLESSED IODASAPH

You did confess the Holy Trinity, O blessed one, illustrious in one essence and indivisible, the Father who knows no beginning, the Son who shares His dominion, the Holy Ghost, the giver of life, One single Godhead.

With the wing of a holy dove, O blessed one, you soared aloft and made haste into the wilderness and awaited the salvation of God, according to the words of the Prophet; and you acted like John and emulated the zeal of Elias, crying aloud to our fathers: 'Blessed art Thou, O God!'

You abandoned countless nations, riches beyond description, and the many-hued adornments of royalty, and you took up your cross upon your shoulders and followed Christ our God, according to His words; and you suffered with Him and were glorified with Him for evermore. Intercede for us also, O worthy one!

The groaning, tears and unspeakable lamentation of the people you left behind—how can human tongue express this? They were as a herd of sheep which have no shepherd, stumbling in the wilderness now that their virtuous pastor has forsaken them, and piteously mourning their grievous lot!

You mounted the chariot of God's service, O righteous one, and armed yourself with the invincible power of Christ. As your shield you had firm faith, and you donned the helmet of truth. With the sword of holiness you wounded Belial and his myrmidons. Wreathed in victory, you cried out to our fathers: 'Blessed art Thou, O God!'

Rejoice, O worthy one, chosen of God, pure offspring of a woman's womb, abode of the most Holy Ghost, dissipator of the obscure murk and spreader of the light of God which shines for all eternity!

Procure us relief from our countless sins by your bold intercession; for you stand before the throne of God, wearing a diadem befitting the multitude of deeds and pious acts which you undertook for the sake of Christ, our God.

Sprinkle my heart, O blessed one, with the dew of divine grace when it is parched by sin; sow in my mind the seed of righteousness; and make fertile the spiritual pasture by the spring of life-giving water.

You did confess the image and glory of the Father who knew no beginning, the Son equal in divine nature, and the Holy Ghost, which shares in the work of creation, O righteous one, and you proclaimed aloud the divine unity of the Holy Trinity and destroyed the error of polytheism.

Neither luxury nor ease nor countless riches could prevail upon you, O blessed one, to forsake the love of Christ our Saviour; nor could the king's fierce wrath shake your resolve, O God-clad one!

The beacons of your words light up the far corners of the land and proclaim your deeds aloud; therefore the Church today with all its sons beautifies your festival day with joy and radiance and exalts those who render honour to you.

When you caught sight, O blessed one, of the crowns indescribably bright which were to be given you as a reward for your deeds, glowing resplendent in the sun of light divine—then your heart was filled with joy and you offered up thanks to God.

Accept now this wreath of praise woven by our feeble lips, O God-crowned monarch Iodasaph, even though it cannot match your sacred nature; for human tongue is incapable of glorifying you fittingly.

Your illustrious festival delights with joy divine the hearts of those who intone their hymn to you with faith; they sound a new trumpet, and with the harp of the spirit as with the psaltery they chant in unison with the sweet voice of the triumphal organ.

You destroyed the error of polytheism, O God-clad one, and proclaimed the divine unity of the Holy Trinity, and the Word born of the Father before all ages, equal with Him in divine power, the offspring of a virgin's womb.

Now boldly beseech God before whose presence you stand, O righteous one, to preserve the churches inviolate, and grant the nation of true believers and their orthodox sovereign victory over the infidel foe, for the exaltation of Christendom.

By the power of your prayers, O worthy one, you drove out of your country the foul devils and all their host, overturned the filthy tabernacles of the idols, and entirely dispelled their reeking fumes which darkened the atmosphere, O blessed one; and you tore away the veil of obscurity from the eyes of men's reason.

Your arms dealt mortal wounds to that wicked deceiver when you raised up the wood of the life-giving Cross and put on the invincible armour of its might; and you shattered his fangs and

A HYMN TO THE BLESSED IODASAPH

dragged from his poisonous jaws countless souls and presented them victorious before God.

You burnt up the evil thorns of godlessness, O worthy one, with the fire of the spirit, and extirpated idolatry root and branch; and you ploughed men's hearts with your God-enlightened tongue and sowed the good seed of the knowledge of God, O blessed one; and those who were drowning in the depths of the sea you steered to safety with the rudder of the cross.

You were aflame with godly zeal, O righteous one, like a fiery furnace, and you burnt up all those that blasphemed the Holy Trinity; and with the lance of the Cross you pierced the hearts of those unseen and evil foes of ours; like Christ Himself you were crowned with victory, and by the arrow of your God-enlightened words you utterly vanquished them.

On this holy festival day, made resplendent by the light of the Trinity, we must commemorate Iodasaph the gallant champion, clapping our hands as we rejoice and sing with spiritual gladness to Christ our God who grants us salvation and has given us so ardent an intercessor.

Filled with the Holy Ghost you fearlessly preached God the Creator of all amid the assembly of the idolaters; for God's grace abode within you from the moment of your birth, O worthy one, and your heart was ablaze with the flame of the love of God which utterly consumed those invisible enemies.

You walked, O blessed one, along the paths of Christ's precepts, guiding the orphans, dispensing justice to the widows and help to the poor and downtrodden, generously enriching the needy, caring for all men as a fond parent, like our Father on high who mercifully protects those whom He has created.

Your mouth is filled, O blessed one, with the divine fragrance of myrrh and spreads spiritual sweetness among the faithful throng; for it flows inexhaustible like the river of Eden and effaces the nauseous smell of sin from the souls of Christ's faithful orthodox believers.

Procure for me, miserable sinner that I am, pardon for my faults and deliverance from eternal torments, that I may escape those dread flames, the impenetrable darkness, the worm that sleeps not, and the many kinds of savage tortures, by your bold intercession with Christ our God.

Heal my soul's wound, O blessed one, wipe away the scar of my sins, rescue me from the poisoned fangs of the devil, and efface pernicious and corrupt instincts from my mind; and unite me with the flock of those that stand on God's right hand by your prayers and intercession, O God-clad, glorious Iodasaph!

BALAVARIANI
OR
THE STORY OF
BARLAAM AND JOSAPHAT

BOOK I

THE LIFE OF THE BLESSED IODASAPH, SON OF ABENES, KING OF INDIA, WHOM THE BLESSED FATHER AND TEACHER BALAHVAR CONVERTED

Grant us thy blessing, O Father!

1. There lived a certain king in the land of India, in the place which they call Sholait,[1] and the name of that king was Abenes. He was a man of strong pagan beliefs, possessing great dominions and armies countless in their numbers, fierce and terrible over all men, victorious over his foes. He was bold, haughty and handsome to the eye and profound in wisdom and judgment. He persecuted and hated the servants of Christ; and his name was Abenes. He was utterly immersed in the pursuit of the pleasures and delights of this world and enslaved by his own passions, and quite unable to exercise any restraint in respect of indulgences which are so pernicious to the soul. There was no desire of his in the world which was not granted to him, except for one thing that was lacking, namely that he had no son.

2. Now the believers in Christ and the holy monks multiplied within his land, many of them renouncing completely all the cares of this world. And they were greatly disturbed by the king's conduct, and the extent to which he surrendered himself to his desires and enslaved himself to the quest of earthly delights. And they began to detest the transitory world and all its affairs. They published abroad its secret vices and snares and the evil consequences which it produced, and declared that the fashion of this world must soon pass away.[2]

And their words reached King Abenes and caused him deep

---

[1] Through a confusion in Georgian script, the manuscript has 'Bolait' here, 'Sholait' elsewhere. The form 'Sholait' reproduces the 'Shawilabat' or 'Sulabat' of the Arabic version.
[2] I Corinthians, vii. 31.

concern, for he said in his heart: 'This hostile campaign of theirs may well produce some revolution in my kingdom and overturn all public order therein!' Therefore he rose in wrath against all the Christians and began to pronounce curses on the men of God and all those who listened to their words. Then by the instigation of the devil he decided to persecute them. And the king set about them with great violence, subjecting them to flogging and torture; and his demented minions brutally assaulted them. And he began to bring idolaters to his court and treat them with great honour, and he exalted their idols and made obeisance before them; and he offered up sacrifices to them and took part in their festive rites. And all the foolish and ignorant populace started serving the idols in company with their king.

Then did the error of idolatry increase in strength, and great woe and affliction fell upon all the churches and upon the faithful, and no one endured but those who sincerely believed Christ with their whole being.

3. After these events, the king happened to ask about a certain knight of his, who was a prominent grandee and distinguished in his sight because of his valour and wisdom. Now this man had left this transitory world behind and become utterly devoted to Christ, and had taken up his abode in the wilderness together with all the other saintly fathers. The king, however, was ignorant of this matter.

When they told the king the news about this grandee, he became very sorrowful and ordered him to be fetched. When they brought him in, Abenes beheld him in the guise of a hermit, dressed in shabby garments just like the men of God. The monarch was filled with wrath and began to scold him angrily and said to him: 'O foolish man, you were honoured and distinguished in my sight! But now you have made yourself ridiculous in company with those fools, destroyed the honourable position which you enjoyed at my court, ruined your reputation, turned yourself into a mockery and made a shameful exhibition of yourself in the sight of the people. You have entered into the way of those lunatics and reprobates, bringing down misfortune upon your family and your sons!'

The man of God answered and said to him: 'Although I have no need to justify myself before you, you should none the less look to your own honour and protect your reason from the assaults of its enemies.'

The king said to him: 'And who is the enemy of my reason?'

That man replied: 'The enemy of your reason is your bad temper, which excites and disturbs it and sets it against those things which are good. Now listen to my word and after you have taken it in, then do whatsoever you desire.'

The king said to him: 'Behold now, I shall desist from my wrath against you. But you must tell me what justification you have to put forward for your own behaviour!'

Then that man said to him: 'Tell me, O king, what is this affair which has excited your wrath against me? Is it for some sin which I have committed against myself, or one against your royal person?'

The king said to him: 'Do you not realize that if you have committed a sin against yourself, then you have sinned against me? For it is my duty to correct those who have gone astray, by means of my justice, true judgment and exhortation, and to safeguard every virtuous quality of my people and punish anyone among them who commits wickedness. If you have perpetrated some evil thing against your own self, which only punishment by me can correct, then do you not realize that you force me to intervene therein? You have the same relationship towards me as any other citizen of my kingdom. If anyone does you a wrong, then it is my duty to award you damages against him; likewise if you commit a wrong against anyone else, then I must award him damages against you. So it is my duty to call you to account now, both on my own behalf and on that of your family and children, for all the havoc which you have wrought upon them.'

The holy man said to him: 'The principle of justice is based on mutual confrontation of witnesses, and nobody can accept the verdict of a tribunal unless public proceedings have duly taken place. Only a judge has the right to deliver a verdict in court. You, O king, have two judges close at hand, one of them being reliable in my eyes, while the other is quite untrustworthy. If the judge who is reliable is going to preside over our case, then justice will be done; but if the one whom I deem untrustworthy presides, then my just cause has no chance of prevailing with him.'

The king said: 'And who are these two judges? Which of them is reliable, and which untrustworthy?'

The man replied and said: 'Reliable in my eyes are your wisdom and understanding, but untrustworthy in my opinion are your anger and your wilfulness.'

The king said to him: 'Behold, I hereby absolve you from the effects of my wrath and wilfulness, and bring into play between us my wisdom and justice, even though it is plain that you have lost your wits. Now tell me all about this affair of yours, and who it is that has led you astray.'

The lover of Christ replied: 'This is how my history began. In the days of my youth I heard a certain saying, and it took root in my consciousness like a seed. I retained a constant memory of this saying within my heart in all my doings, and it sprouted upwards from day to day like a young sapling sprouts up, until this sapling had grown to maturity as a tree and brought forth the fruit which you observe in my person. The saying which I heard was as follows: "The fool imagines the real thing to be unreal, and mistakes the unreal for the real. Whoever fails to comprehend that real thing will be unable to cast out what is unreal."—Now that real thing is the world to come, and the unreal—this present world in which you yourself are ensnared.

'This saying took firm root in my mind and I used to meditate upon it from time to time. When I thought it over, it gave me warning and purified my understanding for the good of my soul. Whenever I was seized by a yearning for earthly pleasures, I thrust them away from me now that I had detected them, before they could corrupt my spirit and my reason. Then the lure of human passions would vanish away, and I would see this world revealed as a furnace of fire blazing all around. That saying exposed to me every snare and pitfall which the world lays to trap all those who are enamoured of it.

'After this I bridled my will, rooted out the sources of lust, and devoted my mind to the study of good and evil. Then the veil of blindness was torn away from my sight, the intoxication of lust vanished away and I became aware of the shame of this transitory world. I surveyed the future, cast my eyes upon the fleeting present and sought experience of man's final destiny, until I had gained sufficient knowledge thereof. Although I made no enquiry, nor did I interrogate it, the world itself revealed and related to me the injuries which it inflicts, not upon its enemies, but upon those who love and cherish it. Then I saw that the purity of the world is nothing but murk; its joy nothing but sorrow; its wealth nothing but poverty; its exaltation nothing but debasement; and its enjoyment nothing but remorse. Nowhere did I discover anyone possessing wealth without incurring worry at the same time, because this wealth could not be utilized without incurring resultant liabilities. Suppose, for instance, a poor man finds a horse. Surely you can see what troubles must beset him? For he needs fodder for it, as well as equipment, a stable, and all kinds of similar necessities. Is there ever any end to this series of human desires, which follow one another in succession? And how can this world avoid being full of sorrow and complaint? There is nobody on earth who can rejoice in his children or his treasures without constantly worrying about them as well. Sorrow and heartache are brought on by the anticipation of impending evils, the onset of sickness or accidental injuries, or else the coming of death itself upon a man's head. The sweetness of self-indulgence turns into bitterness. Delights are rapidly succeeded by depression, from which there is no escape. It follows that it is wrong to involve oneself in the life of this world. This applies particularly to those who have learnt to recognize its snares and delusions. In fact the people who should be the first to detest and flee from the world are those whom the world itself has endowed generously with its gifts, for they are waiting from day to day and from moment to moment for their allotted time to run out; and they tremble for their possessions, or else fear to be hurried away by death when they least expect it. By then it is too late for a man to depart voluntarily from the world which holds him prisoner.

'So now I am denouncing this world to you, O king, and warning you away from it, because it takes away what it gives a man and grudges what it bestows upon him, and afterwards sends him away heavy-laden with sin. It strips a man of his apparel, until even his privy parts are exposed to scorn, and then dresses him up in shame and reproach. It degrades that man whom it has raised up, until his enemies trample him under foot. It deceives those who submit to it, hates those that love it, tricks those that are loyal to it, overturns those that lean upon it, ruins the hope of those that put their trust in it, and turns into bitterness the joy of those that rejoice in it; and nobody can escape in peace once he has fallen in love with it.

'Whenever it makes its voice heard, fools flock to its summons. They carry out its behest, but it turns them into dupes. Today it prepares the gourmet a sumptuous banquet, and tomorrow it turns him over as food for the worms.[1] Today it ministers to one man, tomorrow it will make him minister to others. Today it allows one faction to triumph over their adversaries, and tomorrow it will make their foes gloat over them. Today it makes a man king, tomorrow it will make him slave to another. Today it causes him to stretch out his hand to give, tomorrow it makes him stretch out his hand to beg. Today the world places upon his head a crown fashioned out of precious stones, tomorrow it lays his cheeks prostrate in the grave. Today it bedecks his throat with a necklace, tomorrow it will weigh it down with iron fetters. Today he is beloved by his friends, tomorrow hateful to them. Today the world assembles a chorus to sing his praises, tomorrow it gathers mourners to intone his funeral dirge. Today everyone wants him near, tomorrow the people clamour for his banishment to distant parts, after which he must take up his lodging in the outer gehenna and the flames. The world mourns not those that have passed away, nor does it spare those who remain. It transfers its favours from one to another; when some get out of its clutches, it takes hold of those who remain. It seats evil men in the seats of the virtuous, sets cowards in the place of the valiant, and installs impious men in the abodes of the righteous. It marshals all men on the road to dissolution even before it robs them of their desires. For the people of this transitory world are at enmity with one another, and devour and bite each other like dogs, because they know how short and narrow is their life span, and how rapidly it must pass from them. For this reason they pursue one another, and

---

[1] The Greek renders this phrase as 'It maketh them nought but a gobbet for their enemies (τοῖς ἐχθροῖς)' (Loeb ed., pp. 186-7). The confusion between 'worms' and 'enemies' can be explained only in terms of Georgian, in which language 'worms' are *matlt'a*, and 'enemies', *mtert'a*. S. Qaukhchishvili suggests (*Bizantiuri literaturis istoria*, p. 220) that the redactor of the Greek text had before him a Georgian manuscript with the word given in an abbreviated form, possibly *mtt'a*. At all events, we have here yet another piece of evidence pointing to the derival of the Greek from the longer Georgian recension.

friend persecutes friend, in order to snatch for himself as much as he can before he departs from this life. In this way they overflow with mutual hostility and envy.

'But a man who knows and values the world everlasting places his faith in eternity and in those good things which fall to the saints in time to come. He therefore feels no hostility or envy towards his fellow men, nor does it occur to him to do so. For many are those who desire to dwell in that abode which was promised to them by the only Son of God begotten by His Father, which is in Heaven. These are my brethren and my friends whom I cherish and uphold. But those whom I once deemed to be friends and brothers have turned into my bitterest enemies. This is why I have quitted their company and embarked on the quest for peace.

'Such then is the nature of the world of unreality! But if you wish me to describe to you the world eternal, I will convey its aspect to you just as I have received it. However, no man can appreciate those imperishable treasures of Christ unless he is able to control his own will and intellect.'

The king answered and said to him: 'Accursed man, you have failed to encompass or find anything except for your own downfall, for you have sharpened your tongue for the perversion of the people. If it were not for my pledge to grant you immunity for your utterances, I should forthwith deliver your body to be burned. Arise now and flee away from out of my kingdom!'

So that man departed immediately and withdrew to the wilderness outside to join the holy Fathers.

Then the king became incensed against all the Christian people, and especially against the monks who dwelt in the wilderness, for he said: 'These are pernicious people, who obstruct me in my craving for pleasures and delights!' And on this account he aggravated his persecution of all Christians, while treating the idols with enhanced respect and promoting their ministers to high office.

4. While the king was labouring under this delusion, there was born to him a son, more handsome than any child born in those times. The king was filled with great joy; and he called his name Iodasaph, and said: 'This is what my idols have done for me, because I have exalted them.' And he pressed on increasingly

with wanton revelry along the road to ruin. Then he gathered together a multitude of astrologers, that they might determine the child's future career. And these all declared with a single voice: 'This child shall attain a reign of glory with regal majesty such as nobody has ever achieved in the land of India.'

But among them there was one man, more expert than the others in all branches of wisdom. He declared: 'My verdict is that the glory which this child shall attain is not the glory of this world; but I believe that he is to be a great guide upon the road of truth.'

When the king heard these words, he was filled with sorrow and his joyful mood left him entirely. He ordered a city to be built for his son in a place set apart, and the child lived inside it. And the king detailed trustworthy servants to stay with his son and look after him and afford him every indulgence. When the boy grew up in body and intelligence, Abenes replaced these men by other retainers, warning them not to make any mention in the prince's presence of death, of disease, or of eternity; neither of righteousness nor of sin; neither of old age nor of youth; neither of poverty nor of wealth. If any one of the attendants should fall sick, he was to be speedily removed, so that the boy might not catch sight of him. All these measures the king took so as to prevent the prince from seeing anything which might give him cause for wonderment, and thus lead him to make enquiry about the faith of the Christians.

5. After this King Abenes ordered all Christians and priests, and every believer to be expelled from his dominions. And he sent forth a herald, who proclaimed with a loud voice: 'Thus speaks King Abenes: If after three days I find any of you remaining here, I shall deliver you over to be burned.' So no Christians were left in that land, their very memory being rooted out.

Now the king had in his service a certain counsellor, extremely faithful to him and exalted in honour. This man was virtuous and benevolent, and popular with everybody. However, certain of the king's friends became jealous of him and highly resentful of his superior position, and so they looked out for a suitable moment to encompass his ruin.

One day the king went outside the city for a ride in company with his counsellor, and they arrived at a certain place. The counsellor caught sight of a man lying underneath a tree with his feet grievously wounded and unable to stand up. The nobleman asked him what had befallen him. The man answered: 'I have been mauled by a wild beast. But if you will take me with you, you will find that I shall bring you some profit, if it please God!'

The courtier said to him: 'I shall do this, even if I do not find any advantage in aiding you. But tell me, what precisely is this profit which you say that you will bring me?'

The wounded man answered: 'I am a patcher of words.'

The nobleman enquired: 'How do you patch words?'

The crippled man said: 'If in speech there be any wounds, I can sew them up, so that no damage results from them.'

However, the nobleman paid no heed to this saying, but ordered him to be carried off to his own home and taken care of.

Then the king's intimates hatched a plot against that nobleman, and they said to the king: 'Does Your Majesty not realize that this favourite of yours desires to seize your realm and establish himself upon your royal throne, for which purpose he incessantly stirs up the people? Now if you really want to find out the truth, speak to him in the following terms: "Behold, I am preparing to abandon this world, for it is vain! My aim is to be united with those servants of God whom I have cast forth." —In this way you can test out our allegation, and you will have the chance to see through his hypocrisy.' For those men knew how responsive that nobleman was to any words relating to the life eternal. In their hostility, they were bent on encompassing his doom by this ruse.

The king said to them in reply: 'Unless I find evidence to confirm what you allege, I shall certainly not punish him in any way.'

Then the king summoned his favourite and tested him, saying: 'You know the extent to which my mind has been wrapped up in this world, and the way in which I have spent my days. I see now that I have been toiling away in vain. I am afraid that death may come upon me, and I shall be found completely destitute. Now I wish to strive mightily towards the life eternal, to the same degree that I have striven in the affairs of this world. I see no other alternative but to unite myself to Christ's servants, whom I have subjected to such great persecution. Now what do you say, O faithful adviser of mine?'

When that man had listened to the king's speech, these words inspired him with yearning for Christ, and he burst into tears. And he said to Abenes: 'Live, O king, live for ever! Although eternity is hard to grasp, none the less it is well worth searching for; whereas the transitory world, sweet though it is, is nevertheless to be shunned. It exists, but it is as if it existed not; to those who enjoy it, it brings no joy; to those it pleases, it gives no pleasure. To those on whom it inflicts tribulation, such affliction is of no consequence, for it is but a brief and transitory moment in eternity. Any affliction suffered in the transitory world for God's sake is of brief duration, but its reward in the life eternal lasts for ever. So carry this plan of yours into execution, for it is good that by renouncing this transitory world, you should win in return the world everlasting.'

These words made a painful impression on the king, who was greatly vexed by what this man had said, though he did not declare it to him.

But the counsellor realized that a snare had been laid for him, because he could observe the altered colour of the king's face. So he returned home sunk in deep grief, unable either to fathom the source of the trap into which he had fallen, or to think of anyone who might cure the king's disposition towards him. He passed a sleepless night, and then bethought himself of that man who was a patcher of speech. He summoned him and said to him: 'Once you said to me that you can cure people who have been wounded by words.'

The man replied: 'This is indeed the case! But I trust that you have not been visited by any such affliction?'

The courtier answered: 'All this time I have been serving the king, and never once have I seen him angry towards me, for I have walked before him in faithfulness. But today I have seen him incensed against me, and realized that I am no longer in favour with him.'

The man who was maimed enquired: 'What has transpired between him and yourself?'

The counsellor said to him: 'All I know is that he made a certain declaration to me, and I exhorted him to better things. But my belief is that he was merely tempting me by this conversation.' — And he went on to relate the whole discussion which had taken place between them.

Then the maimed man said to him: 'Following this incident, your speech is sorely wounded indeed! But I will cure it by the grace of God on high. Know this, that the king suspects you of evil designs, and imagines that you are plotting to seize his realm. Certain people advised him to arrange this conversation as a snare for you. Now you must arise tomorrow, shave your head, remove those garments of yours, put on a hair shirt, and enter the king's presence. If the king asks you what this signifies, then tell him: "Behold I have prepared myself for that enterprise to which you called me. For a pampered man like myself, it is easier to die than to endure such a way of life as this, but none the less I do not wish to exist apart from you. Since I have shared in the good things of your reign, it is now my duty to share with you the hardships of this world as well. Just as I have been cosseted by you in the past, so let me now be tormented in company with you, so that we may together become worthy of paradise. Arise now, O king, for your heart has inspired you with an excellent intent." '

The counsellor did just as the maimed one taught him, and all suspicion against him vanished from the king's heart. But Abenes raged violently against the servants of God, and was filled with anger and spite towards them.

6. One day the king went out on a trip round about his city, and caught sight of two men from among the Christians departing from the town. He called them to him and said: 'How comes it that you have made so bold as not to leave my country? Or did you fail to hear the proclamation which my crier addressed to you?'

They answered him: 'Behold, we are on the point of departure from your land.'

The king said to them: 'What is it that has delayed you until now?'

They said: 'The lack of provisions for the journey, for the road that lies before us is long.'

The king retorted: 'He who stands in fear of death does not dally for the sake of provisions.'

The holy men replied: 'Had we been afraid of you, we should

indeed have made haste to go. But to us, death is not something to be dreaded, but to be desired, for thereby we expect to find rest from the troubles of this world. As for the fear felt by those who are in love with this world and prefer it to the life eternal—their fear is not fearful to us, nor can their gladness make us glad.'

The king answered them, saying: 'How can you speak thus? You admit that you are leaving my country at my command. Are you not doing this for fear of death?'

The witnesses of Christ said to him: 'We are fleeing not from fear of death, but to avoid giving you any pretext for venting your evil impulses upon us and providing you with an excuse for committing the godless outrages which you intend to inflict upon us. As for terror of you, this has never entered into our minds.'

At this the king was filled with great wrath and ordered them to be burnt with fire. Thus was their martyrdom accomplished for the sake of Christ, the true God. And a decree was published among all the people that whoever encountered any of the Christians should slay them.

After this all the idolaters arose in turmoil and were encouraged in their evil deeds. They began to vie with the king himself in their murderous and vicious behaviour, intensifying the persecution of all Christians in that country; and they burnt with fire many priests and monks dwelling in the wilderness.

Thenceforth the burning of dead bodies became a custom among the pagans in the land of India.[1] There remained beneath the sway of King Abenes not a single believer known to be a practising Christian, apart from those who dedicated themselves to the creed of the Holy Trinity and the faith which they placed

---

[1] In this passage, the Georgian translator has altered and abridged his text, to the detriment of the meaning. The true significance of this passage can be grasped only by reference to the Arabic version (trans. Rosen, *Povest'* o *Varlaame i Iosafe*, etc., pp. 35-6), where we read: 'And thence self-incineration and the burning of corpses became a custom in the land of the Indians, because of the bliss which the adherents of this creed claimed to be attained through such incineration. And volunteers from among them started burning themselves voluntarily, in order, so they asserted, to attain the same merit as those persons (i.e. the martyrs).' It is clear that the Georgian Christian redactor found the idea of ritual suicide repugnant, and watered it down so that it lost all its original point. Cf. further J. Filliozat, 'La mort volontaire par le feu', in *Journal Asiatique*, CCLI, 1963, fasc. 1, pp. 21-51.

in the true Gospel, to the point of winning the grace of martyrdom for Christ's sake, whereas some others took refuge underground in the catacombs. Many there were also who retained their belief in Jesus Christ in secret, and had not strength to profess it publicly like the others who were martyrs and confessors of the Trinity. And so those pagans subjected the faithful servants of Our Saviour Jesus Christ to much violent abuse and severe tortures.

7. Meanwhile the king's son grew up in the splendour of youth and perfection of body. He was fair to look upon and possessed a firm will and a fertile intelligence. His father took care that he should lack none of that instruction in wisdom and learning which is needful for a king. The only restriction was that nothing should be said to him about the vanity of this transitory world, about the onset of death, or of the inevitable end to which men's life is subject. The reason for this was that the king feared lest such themes might lead the lad to seek out the road of eternity or to investigate the problems of religious faith.

Now the child was most receptive of knowledge, a cherisher of learning, and a seeker out of all words of wisdom, excelling all previous members of that royal house. The king for his part was amazed at the boy's prowess. He did not know whether to feel joy at his intelligence and perfection, or grief and sorrow at the words uttered by the astrologers at the time of his birth.

At length the boy began to remark on his enforced detention within the city, realizing that his father would not allow anyone to visit him, nor permit him to go outside anywhere. And he became filled with resentment on this account. Then he reflected further, and said to himself: 'My father is senior to me and knows all my needs. I have no right to repine, because he is acting in my own best interests.'

So things continued until the prince attained to maturity of wisdom, and said within his heart: 'Even though he is my father, surely I have the right to judge for myself what suits me best. I am grown up now, and I cannot see in what respect I am inferior to my own retainers. Why should I leave them to arrange my affairs for me, and make no effort to find out for myself what is right, as does every normal person?'

Iodasaph's father carried out all his requests, and came to see him at frequent intervals.[1] And the boy determined to take the first opportunity of asking his father about this matter. Then he reflected: 'It is my father who is solely responsible for my confinement. If I consult him, he will not tell me the truth, and I shall only disturb his mind by my curiosity. So I had better try to fathom this question by other means.'

Among the prince's retainers there was one man whom the boy loved more than the others because of his exceptional kindness. Iodasaph thought that this man's help would enable him to discover the true facts about himself. So he began to multiply tokens of affection and respect towards him, singled him out for bestowal of all favours, and promised him still more for the future. The tutor trusted Iodasaph and knew that his word was his bond. When the boy knew that he had gained the man's trust, he approached him confidentially and said to him: 'I have a question to ask you. If you will answer it truthfully, then I assure you that you shall be my friend and beloved above all other men, and you shall always find a haven with me. But if you conceal the facts from me, you will put an end to my affection and cut short your expectations both for the present and for those future times when I expect to inherit my father's kingdom.'

The tutor had complete faith in the prince's integrity and was confident that he would keep secret whatever he told him. So he replied: 'Ask me whatever you like, for my soul has nothing to hide from you.'

The boy said to him: 'Tell me why it is that my father shuts me up here like this and keeps me apart from other people, and other people away from me!'

The tutor answered and said: 'I will relate the story to you and give you the true explanation of this. Now it was those astrologers who persuaded your father to act thus, at the time when your sire was exterminating the servants of God and scattering them abroad from out of his country. The seers declared to the king that you yourself would reach the supreme goal on the road of God's service. Your father was therefore

---

[1] The text says here that his father 'did *not* multiply his visits to him . . .', but the negative is surely an intrusion. The shorter *Wisdom of Balahvar*, trans. D. M. Lang, 1957, has (p. 74): 'But he (i.e. King Abenes) himself used to come frequently, for he loved him.'

afraid that you might incline to do their will and be influenced by their words, and so he cut you off from mankind, in order that you might not cause our nation to adopt an alien creed.'

The lad answered and said to him: 'And what kind of men are those servants of God, to whom my father meted out such harsh treatment?'

Then the tutor told him the whole story of the Christians, and gave him a full account of all their virtues. When the lad had learnt all this, he made him no further answer.

8. When his father next came, Iodasaph said to him: 'I should like you to give me an explanation of a certain problem, which has plunged me into great sorrow and despondency.'

At this his father said to him: 'Ask me whatever question you like, my son!'

The boy said: 'Tell me then, my father and lord, why you have ordained that I should be shut up in this place, and why do you prevent people from visiting me?'

His father replied: 'It is my wish, my son, that you should see nothing to trouble your heart, and I have averted from you all pernicious evils which might mar your pleasure.'

The lad said to him: 'Know, O king, that by the conduct which you have adopted towards me, you have turned all my joys into bitterness, to such an extent that my food is without taste to my palate. You have brought great anguish upon me, because my soul yearns with a great desire for all things that are outside these gates of mine. Now I pray you, father, and beseech you in the name of your regal majesty, to let me out to go abroad and look upon the land; and never will I transgress your command.'

When the king heard these words, he was much grieved; his heart sank as he realized that if he obstructed Iodasaph's will and increased his depression, his son's entire pleasure in life would be soured. So he said to him: 'Son, if you desire to mount your steed and sally forth among men one day, let it be according to your will.' And the king commanded the lad's escorts to take him to beautiful places only, and to ward off everything unpleasant to the human eye; they were to station singers and minstrels along his route, so that his mind should be diverted by such distractions from curiosity about the affairs of the world.

And Iodasaph's retainers acted as the king commanded. So it came about that the king's son made frequent trips outside the town as often as he liked, and wherever he felt inclined.

One day, however, as the lad was going along, he caught sight of two men, one horribly deformed, the other a blind man who was bearing his crippled partner along. His attendants had become careless and omitted to clear these cripples away from his path, as they normally did. When the boy saw them, he was filled with abhorrence at the sight of them, and made enquiry from his retainers concerning them. They said to him: 'These are men who are stricken with infirmity, just as other men also are stricken. That first man's deformity springs from some internal ailment, whereas the other's blindness is also the result of disease.'

The boy said to them: 'Is this fate common to all men?'

They answered: 'Not to all, only to certain ones.'

Again the youth asked them: 'Can one foretell on whom this calamity shall fall, as well as knowing who will be spared from it?'

They answered him: 'Some it attacks, and others escape it; but this cannot be determined by human volition.'

The lad said to them: 'So there is nobody who can be really assured that it will not befall himself?'

They replied: 'There is no one.'

Then he began to brood and to meditate; he was disturbed in mind and his complexion changed colour, and he returned home weighed down with melancholy.

On another occasion, Iodasaph took a ride in the open air and saw an old man stricken with years, bent double to the ground. The colour of his face was black, his hair white, his flesh shrivelled; not a single tooth was left in his mouth, his speech was incoherent, and he crawled upon his hands and knees. The sight of this old man revived the prince's terror and he began to interrogate his associates about him.

They told him: 'This is a man who is ancient of days, on whom increasing age has brought decreasing strength, until he has reached the condition in which you see him. Henceforth he will decline still further every day.'

The lad asked: 'And does this fate befall every human being?'

They answered: 'Yes, it does, unless death forestalls it.'

The youth asked: 'What is the next stage after this?'
They replied: 'After this, death will carry him off.'
The lad enquired: 'And when does a man arrive at this state?'
They told him: 'After eighty years, or sometimes a hundred.'
'What is a year?' the lad asked them.
'Twelve months,' they said.
'And what is a month?' the youth enquired.
They told him: 'Thirty days.'
'After all this,' the lad asked, 'is there no reprieve from death, nor any means of avoiding this senile state, followed by death?'
They answered him: 'There is no escape from it!'
The boy said: 'As for those afflictions of which I have seen examples, namely deformity and blindness, is it a fact that nobody is guaranteed immunity from their attack, however brave he may be?'
They answered him: 'The truth is as you state it.'
'Does this apply equally all over the world?' asked the boy.
They replied: 'Yes, that is indeed so.'[1]
Then the lad said: 'No longer is there any sweetness in this transitory life now that I have seen these things; and no one has any respite from sudden or gradual death. Gradual and sudden death are close in league together. Day follows hard on day inside the month, the year follows hard upon the heels of the month. Soon the years themselves must pass away, to drain a man's life from him, even if he succeeds in living out the full span of human existence.'

Then the prince departed, fretting over these matters and ceaselessly dwelling on these topics in conversation and within his heart. Thenceforth he began to repine and mope, and set no value on the delights of this world. His depression grew more acute every day. None the less, Iodasaph took trouble to humour his father. Whenever he met him, he put on a cheerful and carefree manner, lest his father should learn the reason for his melancholy and prevent him henceforth from leaving the city.

---

[1] These three examples of human decay seen by Iodasaph correspond to three of the Four Omens of Buddhist tradition, where they take the form of a man worn out by age, a sick man, and a dead body. The Fourth Omen leading directly to the Buddha's Great Renunciation is Gautama's encounter with a mendicant monk. This monk appears later on in our Christian story in the shape of the Christian hermit Balahvar (Barlaam), who converts Iodasaph to the way of truth.

Whenever he met anyone capable of intelligent conversation, he would listen attentively to what he said, hoping to hear from somebody a message of truth which would lift the gloom from his heart.

One day he summoned his tutor and said to him: 'Do you not know of any person here who follows a faith different from ours?'

The tutor replied: 'There used to be some men living here, about whom I told you previously, and who were called Christians and servants of God—men who hated this world and its delights and sought, or so they claimed, for the eternal kingdom. Their faith does not resemble our faith, nor does their conduct resemble our conduct. But the king was hostile towards them and expelled them from our country: many of them he exterminated by various forms of torture and by fire, as I have already explained to you. At present I know of none of them remaining in our land.'

When the tutor had described their deeds to him, the young prince's interest was aroused and he longed to see these men for himself. He was like a man who has lost some treasure and is desperately hunting for it. He made a parade of his detestation and hate for the transitory world, exclaiming: 'Abominable in my sight are the pleasures of this earth!' And he spurned all the ways of the world and its devotees, until his reputation was spread in all places; and all those who heard about Iodasaph praised God, who is made manifest in the Trinity and glorified in Unity, whose majesty belongs to the Father, the Son and the Holy Ghost, now and for ever and to all eternity, Amen.[1]

[1] Here follows a note by the scribe: 'O Christ, have mercy on David, Amen.'

BOOK 2

CONCERNING THE ARRIVAL OF OUR HOLY AND BLESSED FATHER BALAHVAR, WHO CONVERTED THE KING'S SON TO THE RELIGION OF CHRIST

9. Now this report reached a certain man who loved God and was graced by the habit of the monastic order, and filled with the Holy Spirit and all manner of wisdom; his name was Balahvar and he dwelt in the land of Sarnadib.[1] He heard about the prince, and learnt that he thirsted and yearned for the faith of Jesus Christ Our God. So he embarked on a ship and arrived in that kingdom, where he discarded his monastic attire and donned the garb of a merchant. He began to cultivate local society and frequently visited the king's court, as was the general custom, until he had got to know the people there and their several relationships with the king and his son.

He also found out about the special status of the prince's tutor. One day he gained a confidential interview with him and said: 'I am a foreigner come from a far country. In my possession is a treasure of great price which I have kept hidden from men. I have resolved to reveal it to no one but yourself, because I have confidence in your virtue and intelligence, that you will do me the favour of keeping this business a complete secret.'

The tutor answered: 'You can trust me to do your bidding with complete honesty. I will reveal this matter to nobody but the person whom you yourself name.'

Balahvar said to him: 'The treasure I possess is finer than red brimstone, since it restores sight to blind men's eyes and hearing to the deaf, makes the dumb speak, cleanses the lepers, causes the lame to arise and walk, strengthens the ailing, enriches those that are in want, and cures all ailments; it grants victory over the foe, drives out devils from the possessed, and furnishes a man with all his heart's desire.'

---

[1] A corruption of the Arabic 'Sarandib', i.e. Ceylon. The transposition of the vowel 'a' and consonant 'n' is particularly characteristic of a misreading of Arabic script.

The tutor said to him: 'You do not look a fool to me, O stranger, though your words sound like the prattle of some loquacious babbler. What you tell me is unlike anything I have heard before. Still, I find it hard to regard you as a liar when I contemplate the gravity of your outward demeanour. So tell me now: What is this treasure of which you speak? Show it to me, let me have a look at it! If it is of regal quality, I shall inform the king's son about it. It would be unwise for me to praise a thing to him beyond measure, so that when he came to examine it, he would not find it a match for my account of it.'

Balahvar the wise said to him: 'You ask me to show it to you —but no one has the power to see it unless he possesses two qualities: soundness of eyesight and a body pure of sin. If any man who is dim of vision and steeped in sin should catch sight of it, the light of his eyes will be extinguished and he will lose his wits as well. Now I am a physician, and I can see that your eyesight is dim. I am afraid that the brilliance of this thing will quench the light of your eyes. But I have heard of the prince's exemplary conduct and holy way of life, kept pure from all evil ways; and he is still a lad and sharp of eye. And so I place my trust in God, that the prince may be given power to look upon this treasure of mine.'

The tutor replied: 'I have taken note of all that you have said. I am a man polluted by sins, and can no longer aspire to set eyes upon that treasure. Furthermore, my eyesight, as you observe, is no longer sharp, so I have no wish in this transitory existence to look at it at all. However, I believe that you are speaking the truth and not lies.'

Balahvar declared to him: 'Indeed I am telling you the truth. Have faith in me, and do not be afraid to make these things known to the king's son, for he is worthy of them. One who holds an official position such as yours should certainly not hide so fine a treasure from him; and if you do tell him about it, then you will win for yourself increased favour and honour in his sight, greater than that enjoyed by any of your colleagues.'

After this the tutor went in before the prince and told him everything he had heard from Balahvar the wise. Now the boy longed for human company, hoping that he might hear from someone's lips words profitable to the soul. When Iodasaph had listened to the tutor's story with its miraculous account of the treasure, his mind sensed that in the person of Balahvar he would find what he desired. So he ordered him to be brought in privately, together with his treasure.

10. So Balahvar was escorted in, holding a small casket in which he pretended that a jewel was contained. When he made his appearance before the king's son, he offered Iodasaph greetings and began to utter prayers for his prosperity, as it is fitting to do before kings. The prince likewise received him with honour and enquired cordially after his health. Then Iodasaph told the tutor to give up his seat to Balahvar and leave the room. When he had gone out, he told Balahvar to sit down and said to him: 'Show me this treasure which you have brought with you.'

Balahvar answered and said to him: 'It would be terrible if any accident befell you through negligence on my part, for my treasure does really possess those properties which your tutor described to you. No one is capable of setting eyes on it except a man of pure and innocent character, with a fully-developed intelligence. If anyone feeble of wit should see it, he would lose what brains he has and the sight of his eyes to boot. So now I propose to test you in conversation and to hold speech with you, and if I find you qualified to look upon it, I shall show it to you, for I have brought it especially for you and for no one else. I place my hopes in God, that you have attained the ability to look upon it; you shall certainly succeed in this if it be God's will. For during this audience, O prince, you have received and welcomed me, an unknown stranger, with the same exemplary courtesy which you accord to the grandees of your palace!'

Iodasaph answered and said: 'This is because I am most confident that your visit will prove worthwhile, and that I shall receive from you that which my heart desires.'

FABLE THE FIRST

The Trumpet of Death: The Four Caskets

11. Balahvar said to him: 'Exceptional though your kindness is, there is nothing amazing about it. For once upon a time there lived a certain pious king, who was virtuous and sought after righteousness. When he was passing along the road one day with

a throng of followers, he caught sight of two men clad in tattered garments made up from rags salvaged from rubbish heaps; and their sallow complexions testified to their poverty and need. But the king recognized them: at their sight, he swiftly dismounted from his horse before them, embraced their necks and accorded them great honour and respect. When his companions saw this, they strongly resented the king's conduct and considered his behaviour most ridiculous, for their monarchs were quite unaccustomed to behave in this fashion. Not daring to reproach the king themselves, they went to see his brother, who habitually spoke his mind frankly to him. The courtiers told him what the monarch had done, and urged him to admonish the king not to do such a thing again. So the king's brother went to him and repeated what those people had told him. When he had finished speaking, the king answered him in noncommittal terms which left him in doubt whether His Majesty had paid any heed to his representations, or whether he was merely vexed by them.

'Now it was the custom in that kingdom when the king was angry with anyone and intended to put him to death, that he would send a herald, known as the herald of death, who would make a loud noise before the gates of the victim's house, and blow upon a trumpet. When the master of the house heard this, he would know for certain that he was soon to die, and all the people would know it too. So after a few days, the king ordered the herald of death to go and sound a fanfare at his brother's gates. The herald went forth and made a great noise and blew the trumpet of death before his door. When the king's brother heard its blast, he despaired of his life and made his last will and testament; and his household began to weep and tear their hair. Then he donned his own burial garment and went with his wife and children to the royal palace, all shedding tears of despair and uttering loud laments; and they sprinkled ashes upon their heads.

'The king ordered them to be brought into his presence. His brother wept and implored mercy. Then the king said to him: "O fool and slow of understanding, how comes it that you were so prostrated with terror at your brother's herald when he sounded the signal of death before your gates? Surely you know that your brother and his herald are but mortal men created by

Almighty God, incapable either of hastening the fulfilment of His will towards them, or of averting their own destiny? You know that you have not committed any crime against your brother to render you liable to the death penalty. Why then were you astonished at my dismounting and falling down before those who are heralds of Our Lord God and Saviour Jesus Christ, who remind me that I shall meet Him face to face, and expound to me the words of His gospel? I am well aware of my many sins. Lo then, it was to reprove your folly that I played you this trick, even as I shall shortly convict of vanity those that prompted your reproof of me." And the king forgave his brother, after giving him this salutory lesson.

12. 'Then the king ordered four caskets to be made. Two of them he had inset with gold and silver and carbuncles and precious stones. He had these ones stuffed with dead men's bones and all manner of unclean refuse, which is loathsome to men's senses. Then he secured them with golden clasps. After this, he had the two other caskets smeared with tar and pitch. And he filled their interior with carbuncles and precious stones and all manner of sweet perfumes which delight men's senses. These he fastened with bits of old rope. Then the king called for those courtiers of his who had been scandalized by the respect shown by him to the saintly mendicants. When they had taken their seats before him, he had the two sets of caskets brought in, both the gilded ones and the others as well, and invited them to appraise them. Concerning the two gilded ones they said: "Our minds cannot fathom their true value, for they deserve to be receptacles of all manner of precious treasure; as for those two pitch-smeared ones, we feel that these unsightly objects can have no value worth mentioning."

'At this the king said: "Of course! Such is bound to be your verdict and assessment, for you look at nothing but people's outward appearance!" Then he ordered the two caskets inlaid with gold to be opened. And the assembled company shrank from the loathsome trash which they contained, and the stench from it filled their nostrils.

'The king remarked: "This is the image of all those people who deck themselves out with fine raiment and gold, but within are full of stupidity, boredom, falsehood, filth and all manner of unclean elements, more nauseating even than any refuse which this world produces."

'Next he had the two pitch-smeared caskets opened up, and the mansion was lit up with the radiance of the jewels, and the company was delighted with the savour of perfume.

'The king said: "This is the image of those holy men, my veneration for whom scandalized you so intensely when you surveyed their shabby raiment with your outward eye. For my part, I was surveying their inward nature through the eyes of my mind."

'Then the courtiers declared that they had profited greatly by this parable, and knew now that the king had acted rightly.'

And Balahvar concluded: 'This is a semblance of you, O king's son, for you have granted me honour in return for the joyous tidings which you expect to hear from me.'

13. Then the prince arose from his throne and said in his heart: 'It appears that here indeed is my heart's desire, for which I was seeking.' Turning to Balahvar, he exclaimed: 'Exceeding good is your discourse and manifest is the truth of it. I take it that this in fact is that very treasure which you keep hidden, for it strengthens my heart, lightens my eyes and fortifies my understanding. If the matter stands as I believe, pray give me confirmation of this. If you have something else to tell me besides what I have heard, I shall be very satisfied to receive it instead of the jewel. For you have greatly enlightened my mind by your discourse and torn away the veil of melancholy from my heart. So now tell me an allegory about goodness.'

FABLE THE SECOND

The Sower

Balahvar said: 'A certain sower went forth, gathered up good seed and began to sow. And some seed fell by the roadside, and straightway the birds pecked it up; some fell upon the rock, on which there was just a little soil and moisture, and sprouted up, but when its roots reached the arid surface of the rock, they withered away; and some fell among thorns, and when it sprouted up the thorns choked and killed it; but some fell upon good ground free from tares, and although there was but little of it, it sprouted up and brought forth much fruit.

'Now the sower is the giver of wisdom, Christ Our God, and the good seeds are the words of truth uttered by His sacred mouth. The ones which fell by the roadside, so that the birds pecked them up, are those which are heard by the ear, but pass the heart by; and the ones which fell on the moist spot and sprouted up, and then withered away because of the aridity of the rock, are those which a man hears and finds congenial, and acknowledges as true for a brief moment, but then fails to grasp with his mind. But those which sprouted up and were about to bring forth fruit, only to be choked by the thorns, are those words which a man cherishes, but when it comes to putting the ideas which he has accepted into effect, his ambitions stifle and choke them. But the seed which sprouted up and brought forth much fruit is that which the eye will harvest, the heart gather in, and the mind bring to perfection; and it will conquer lusts and cleanse the heart from sins.'

The king's son said to him: 'I place my hope in Christ, that whatever seed you implant in me may sprout up and bring forth much fruit. Now convey to me the likeness of the transitory world, and how it deludes those who cherish it.'

FABLE THE THIRD

The Man and the Elephant

14. Balahvar said to him: 'This transitory life and all that cherish it resemble a man pursued by a raging elephant, which cornered him inside a fearsome abyss. As he fell down inside it he found two branches growing out over the precipice, so he hung on to them, and then managed to establish some sort of foothold. When he looked around him, he descried two mice, one white and the other black, which never ceased to gnaw at the roots of those trees on which he hung. Then he looked down into the chasm and noticed a dragon, which had parted its jaws and was intent on swallowing him up. And on the ledge on which his feet rested he discerned four heads of asps projecting from the cliff. Then he lifted up his eyes and saw that a little honey was dripping from the branches of the tree, and he began to eat it. And its flavour and sweetness so entranced him that he

no longer worried about the perils which beset him and the fact that he might be bitten to death at any moment. As for the branches on which he was suspended, he saw the tree's roots being gnawed away by the mice and—most dangerous of all—the dragon lying in wait to swallow him up, but all this failed to trouble him in the slightest.

'Now that elephant is the harbinger of death, which pursues the sons of Adam, and the abyss is the world, full of all manner of evil and pernicious snares. The two branches are a man's life span and the two mice—one white and the other black—are the days and nights that fret away at it incessantly, and suddenly sever the thread of a man's life. The four asps signify the four elements from which a man's body is constructed, and when a single one of them is destroyed, life comes to an end. The dragon which opened its jaws and longed to swallow him up, is the image of hell, into which the lovers of this world enter after their death. And those few drops of honey are the brief delights of this world, by which it deceives those who are led astray by the sweetness of corruption.'

15. The king's son said: 'This comparison is just and the parable truly remarkable! Behold, you have revived my spirits by this discourse of yours. Now tell me an allegory about this vain world and its devotees—those people who are infatuated by its charms and contemptuous towards the better life.'

FABLE THE FOURTH

The Man and his Three Friends

Balahvar said: 'This world and those who love it resemble people delighting in thorns smeared with honey, and spurning the blossoms which fill the garden with fragrance, which is the rejection of the world.—Now this is like the case of a certain man who had three friends. One of these he loved more than anybody else;[1] [and he thought about him day and night and

---

[1] At this point one leaf (fol. 35) is missing from the Jerusalem manuscript. However, this fable is present in the shorter Georgian *Wisdom of Balahvar* (trans. Lang, 1957, pp. 82-3), as well as the Greek, Arabic and other main recensions, from which the missing passage has been reconstructed for the purpose of this translation.

exposed himself to risk and hazard for his sake, not wavering in his devotion towards him nor hesitating to sacrifice for his friend both his life and his possessions. Now the second friend occupied a lower place than the first in his affections, but was none the less his intimate friend and boon companion, so that he esteemed and cherished him, rendered him services, gave him presents, and ceased not to exert himself on his behalf. But the third friend he slighted and neglected and found tedious, so that he devoted to him only an infinitesimal share of his efforts, love and property, scarcely ever paying him a visit and then only on rare occasions.

'All at once there befell that man one of those misfortunes when a man has need of friends and trustworthy allies. The king's sheriffs arrived to hale him off before the royal presence, and the man ran in terror to his first friend and said to him: "You know how much I love you, what sacrifices I have made for your sake, and what risks I have incurred on your behalf. Now today I have desperate need of your help, seeing that they are dragging me away for trial. What are you prepared to do to help me?'

'The other replied: "I am no friend of yours, but have companions of my own with whom I must needs make merry. All I can do is to supply you with a couple of garments, though these will not be of much use to you."

'Then he ran panic-stricken to his second friend whom he loved and cherished and said to him: "What can you do for me, for I have not ceased from exerting myself on your behalf? Behold, today is the moment when I have most need of you, for they are hauling me off for trial!"

'That friend replied: "I have no time for you today, because I have enough troubles of my own to attend to. Go your way, and know that I am no longer any friend of yours. However, I will accompany you a few steps, and then return to look after my own affairs."

'Finally that man had recourse to the third friend, whom he had despised in the days of his prosperity, and said to him][1] with a shamefaced expression: "I scarcely dare open my lips to plead

---

[1] At this point we resume our translation from the Jerusalem manuscript, in the edition of Professor Ilia Abuladze.

for your help, but I am driven to have recourse to you in my grievous misfortune, in the hope that you will afford me solace in my hour of need."

'Then this man answered him joyfully and said: "I am your friend, and I have stored up the memory of your little kindnesses to me. And now I will repay you with interest. Have no fear, for I will accompany and intercede for you in your trouble, and not deliver you into the hands of your enemies nor betray you. Cheer up now, for there will surely follow a happy issue from your misfortune."

'Then that man exclaimed: "I do not know which I should repent of more deeply—my excessive coldness towards my true friend, or my exaggerated fondness for those two false ones!"'

The king's son said to him: 'This excellent parable appeals to me greatly. Pray explain its true meaning to me.'

Balahvar said to him: 'That first friend is the love of money, which men hoard up. For the sake of their cherished possessions, they pay no heed to death, nor do they hesitate to incur all manner of trouble and effort for their sake. But when death is at hand, a man's riches avail him nothing, apart from providing a couple of shrouds to serve as his winding sheets. This is all the return they render him, after which they find another friend with whom to make merry. Now the second friend is wife and children, to whom men are passionately attached, making all manner of effort and exhausting both mind and body for their sake; but on the day of his death, they can avail a man nothing, except that they will undertake a short journey as far as his tomb and then turn back to look after their own affairs and bury his memory in oblivion. But the third friend, the one that was completely neglected, is the company of good deeds: love, mercy, faith, trust, holiness and similar virtues which can accompany us and deliver us on the day of judgment, returning with interest whatever little kindnesses we have rendered. This then is the image of this world and those that love it.'

16. The king's son said to him: 'I realize that you are making the whole truth known to me, and it is perfectly clear to my mind. Tell me now how the world exercises its deceit, and how a person can elude it.'

PLATE I

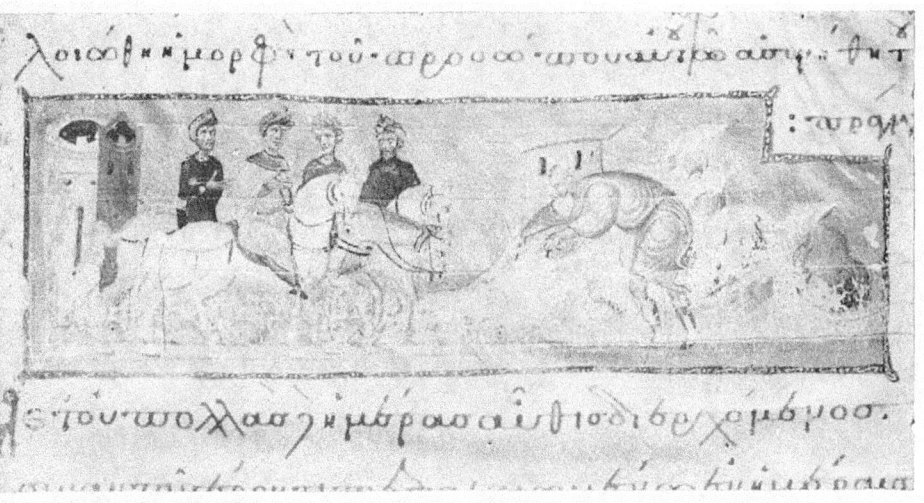

Iodasaph meets the old man

Balahvar reveals himself to Iodasaph

PLATE II

The trumpet of death

The Fable of the Four Caskets

The Man and the Unicorn

FABLE THE FIFTH

The King for One Year

Balahvar said to him: 'I will tell you, O prince, how to elude worldly temptation.—This calls to mind the citizens of a certain town, whose annual custom it was to bring in a foreigner who knew nothing of their traditions, and set him up as king within their city. And the benighted man would imagine that his reign over them was permanent for all time. So he would begin to eat and drink and be merry with never a care, for the citizens let him follow his own will and pleasure throughout his year of office, without giving him any inkling of their peculiar ways. But when one year had expired, the citizens would invade his mansion, strip him bare and drive him out naked and ashamed into exile in a foreign country. There the king would be left without food, drink or clothing or any form of solace. And thus his previous luxury and merrymaking would turn into repentance and woe.—Such then was their regular custom.

'Now on one occasion they elected a certain man to be king over them, according to their custom. But this man was a person of intelligence. When they set him up as their ruler, he realized that he was but an alien in their midst and placed no trust in them. So he looked for some man who could counsel him how to act towards his subjects. When he had found a reliable man who knew the custom of those citizens, the king confided his problem to him, mentioning his alien status among them and his lack of confidence towards them. Then that man gave him the following advice: "I will tell you how you should proceed. Start by removing as much as you can from the treasure houses under your control—gold, precious stones and choice carbuncles, and all manner of valuables—and send them off for safe custody to that foreign land whither they relegate their kings after stripping and banishing them. When they drive you out, as their custom is, you will find everything which you have sent on in advance, and be able to enjoy it all the more in complete security, without suffering the regret and sorrow which have afflicted your royal predecessors."

'So the king did as that sensible and wise man advised him. When his year had expired, the citizens rose against him, stripped him, and banished him to that foreign land according to their custom. There he recovered everything which he had sent on ahead. From now on he passed his time in merrymaking and luxury without stint, and had no more fear or concern for those fickle citizens; nor did he have to rue the prospect of a lifetime of destitution.

'Now that city is this vain world, and the citizens are the devils who control this world of darkness.[1] These entice us with manifold allurements, and mankind in its folly imagines its enjoyment to be everlasting. Now I pray to Christ to make me resemble that good counsellor, and you to be like that wise and sensible king who placed no trust in those foreign citizens and was not duped by the regal status which they conferred upon him. Henceforth you too must strive to escape such terrible snares as these, for I have shown you the way and you have no excuse for further negligence.'

17. Iodasaph said: 'I place my trust in Christ, the Son of God, and in your holy prayers, that I may be the sort of man you have in mind. Justly have you exposed to me the shortcomings of this world. Now I know that the semblance of this world is transient. My own personal experience has already inspired me with contempt for it, but your discourse has strongly increased my detestation of it. Tell me now, does every man of your country understand the affairs of this world as you do, and speak of them in the same terms as you yourself?'

Balahvar answered: 'No; but I belong to that company of persons who are devoted to Christ, the God of all men. We have abandoned this world to those who are fond of it, and have withdrawn to remote desert places and mountains to practise the exercises and customs of the monks, which is the similitude and image of the angels. Originally we were subjects of your father. But when he learnt of our feats and assemblies, he was horrified and took fright, for he imagined that we were plotting to seize his temporal authority. His opinion about us was derived from his courtiers, who shared in his luxury and regal majesty. It was they who incited him to banish us, kill us and burn us with fire. And your father did so, because we despise him and have selected for ourselves a greater king, namely Jesus Christ.

[1] Cf. Ephesians, vi.12.

Iodasaph enquired: 'Why then did the whole nation turn hostile towards you, and ready to slander your companions?'

Balahvar replied: 'Their hostility was indeed quite as great as you have heard say. But how could their slander affect a class of men who speak and lie not; who pray and sleep not; who fast and feed not; who suffer privation and falter not; and who give thanks for what is good and feel no jealousy for those things on account of which mankind is jealous?'

Iodasaph said: 'In what respect are such men free of jealousy?'

Balahvar answered: 'The ascetics feel no jealousy either in regard to possessions or to wives and children, and nobody need entertain any fear that they harbour designs on either their wealth or their womenfolk. Human enmity has its sole basis in men's struggle to amass treasure, each one more than his neighbour.'

FABLE THE SIXTH

Dogs and Carrion

18. Iodasaph said to him: 'How is it then that people have conspired together to treat you and your comrades so despitefully? For it is clear that men are themselves at loggerheads regarding their own affairs!'

Balahvar answered him: 'It is because seekers after worldly bliss, however envious and hostile they may be to one another, yet confine their enmity to transitory matters. Towards the believers who serve Christ Our God, however, they behave like dogs of various hues, gathered together from divers places and crowding round some carrion and biting at each other. But as soon as they catch sight of a wayfarer passing by, they stop snapping at each other and all with one accord co-operate in attacking him, for they imagine this man to be coming along with designs on their carrion. This idea of theirs arises from their greed and gluttony. As soon as they notice that man's alien presence among them, they make common cause against him, although they were previously at enmity; and they fail to realize that this carrion of theirs is quite valueless to him.

'Such are the lovers of this world, who have chosen it in preference to paradise. They devour one another and shed their blood for its sake; and in this occupation they waste their days, engrossed in the quest after worldly honour and glory, and deathly envy dwells constantly within their hearts. But when they observe those people who are foes to this world and have no care other than to free themselves from it and have no share in their worldly ambitions, then they imagine those persons are setting a trap for them with ulterior motive; for they attribute to the believers in Christ their own treacherous mentality. This is why they conspire together to maintain enmity towards us; they have adopted this attitude because of their lack of understanding, and have persuaded your father that the sole aim of our company is to foment opposition to his regime. Your father has failed to grasp the true facts, namely that the majesty and glory of his royal estate are low and despicable in the eyes of true believers in Our Saviour Jesus Christ, and most of all to genuine monks, who view his life of luxury as something detestable, and are perpetually scandalized to see how his mind has become dominated by the delights of this world.'

FABLE THE SEVENTH

Physician and Patient

19. Iodasaph said to Balahvar: 'Enough of mere words! Begin to proclaim the message of salvation!'

Balahvar replied: 'When a skilled physician sees a body deranged by grievous ailments and wishes to restore it to health, he does not attempt to build up the flesh by gorging it with food and drink. For he knows that if food and drink are mixed with the corrupt humours, they would disagree with the system and harm the body rather than doing it any good. But those through whom God in His providence operates the conquest of disease will rather impose a regime and administer medicine.

'As soon as the distemper and the corrupt humour have been expelled through God's grace, then it is that they will nourish the patient with food and drink; and straightway the palate will acquire a relish for good cheer, and he whose death God wishes to avert will be restored to health.'

20. Iodasaph said to him: 'Tell me, holy father Balahvar, how did you begin to attain this degree of austerity, and how did you embark on the monastic career?'

The holy Balahvar answered: 'When I was still absorbed in this worldly life, I observed the vicissitudes to which people were subject in their business and family affairs, appearing as if caught in a snare before the onset of disaster. When I noticed how short a time they spent in enjoyment and what a tremendous effort they made to obtain it, I repented of my previous folly and excess of error. Accordingly I set out to replace my blindness by righteousness and to cultivate my reason. Lifting up my eyes, I analyzed my own nature, that I might restore my depraved character to its pristine purity and attain to the estate of the holy fathers. I trained my heart day by day, until it was converted to love Christ and yearn for virtue. Then I began to wean my desires and appetites away from their accustomed habits, and got them under my own control. I found it hard to submit to the laws of the faith and the delights of endurance until the murk of darkness was stripped away from my eyes and the intoxication of futility dissipated, and I could boldly resist all pleasurable allurements. Then I beheld the shamefulness of the way of life which I now eschewed. I realized clearly how superior was the way of life which I had now taken up, my yearning for which waxed all the greater. I treated myself like a shepherd tends his flock, meting out pasture to the obedient and the disobedient for them to graze on according to their deserts. Thus did I govern my own nature, sometimes rewarding it for its endurance, sometimes chastening it for its lack of perseverence, until I had fortified those qualities which I held dear and eliminated those which I deemed detestable.'

Iodasaph enquired 'This message which you and your associates proclaim and preach—is it something which you yourselves sought out by your own wisdom and knowledge, and on discovering it to be true, adopted it in preference to all other codes of conduct? Or did God Himself make His voice heard to you, eliciting this response from you?'

Balahvar declared: 'This matter is loftier and more exalted than the wisdom of this world. Had this beauteous vocation of monasticism been established by worldly wisdom, its path would have been easy and broad. Had it been created by human ingenuity, it would have invited people to love this world too, with all its allurements and delights. But in fact this is something alien to the world, being proclaimed publicly by the true

Godhead, and able to overcome all forces hostile to God and crush temptations which lead to self-indulgence; it is a creed which is hostile to pleasure and numbs the enjoyment of it, and summons men to obey the will of Jesus Christ Our Lord. It is manifest that this is an ordinance of the King of heaven and earth, who reigns jointly with the Father and the Holy Ghost, for it is more sublime than any utterance of men and loftier than human nature and vision. God revealed this holy creed by the mouth of the holy apostles and prophets to certain men, and to these were granted faith and salvation; verily were they confirmed through the holy apostles in a life wondrous and like unto that of the angels.'

FABLE THE EIGHTH

The Sun of Wisdom

21. Iodasaph said: 'What is that wisdom which is praised for its excellence and perfection and filled with every honourable power? And how is it that not everyone benefits from it?

The holy Balahvar said: 'The image of that wisdom resembles the sun, which shines upon all mankind, great and small alike; no one is debarred from deriving benefit from it, nor is anyone who so wishes hindered from enjoying its warmth or stretching out his hand towards its beams. But if someone chooses not to enjoy it, the sun is not to blame. The same applies to wisdom among men until the day of the resurrection, for its light shines upon all men like the light of the sun, and is readily accessible to all.

'However, men surpass one another in this, just as one pearl is worth many hundred shillings and another only two shillings.[1] But whoever shall seek after wisdom and find it and shall cherish that spiritual wisdom, fulfilling it not with lip-service only but in deed, that man shall be like a pearl of great price; and if someone shall fail to discover that great pearl, then even a little one, however insignificant, is not without value.'

Iodasaph said: 'Is there any form of wisdom which its seekers fail for a long time to attain, but then light upon by some happy chance?'

Balahvar replied: 'This is the case with most men engaged in

---

[1] The Arabic refers to the coin in question as a *dirhem*, the Georgian as a *dangi*.

the pursuit of wisdom, for wisdom falls into a number of categories. Some of these are close at hand and straightforward, others are remote and hard of access; some are evident, and others concealed; some are conspicuous and others profound. Wisdom is like springs of water, some trickling gently from the depths of the earth and others gushing into the air like fountains to the height of a man or the length of a lance; some flow out of profound chasms, and others from waterless deserts in the depths of which no moisture can be descried. Then again, springs of water are of many different qualities. Some are shallow, sweet and agreeable; some suffer from being remote, turgid and in scant supply; others combine the virtues of being pleasant, near at hand and abundant in their flow.'

22. Iodasaph said: 'Do you know of anyone besides yourselves who has been urging people to quit this transitory world and spurn its pleasures?'

Balahvar replied: 'In this country we are alone in this ministry, and apart from us there is no one. In other lands there are righteous men who profess to propagate the true faith in their own language and to preach the message of truth. But many of their projects have ended in ruin. Some of them fulfil the divine word in their conduct, but others behave in a way quite incompatible with their professed beliefs. Most of them are in fact deluded[1] both in conduct and in doctrine, and their doings have nothing in common with ours.'

Iodasaph said: 'How can one be assured that the gospel you preach is truer than theirs? How did you and they gain knowledge of the truth?'

Balahvar answered him: 'Every true doctrine is vouchsafed to man by Jesus Christ, for He called on all men to follow Him. Some heard His voice and responded to it, adopting in its entirety the doctrine and creed which He preached. And when it was ripe, they offered the fruit thereof as a sacrifice to God, as was fitting. But some there were whose characters lacked fortitude and perseverance, so that they faltered, languished and perished. Now what common ground can there be between a preserver and a destroyer, a builder and a wrecker, between one

---

[1] In the Jerusalem manuscript, the scribe has added a marginal note here: 'By "deluded persons", the blessed Balahvar is referring to heretics.'

who stands fast and one who abandons the struggle? Nobody must proclaim the gospel message unless it be based on the preaching of truth! Their new-fangled heresies have set up a barrier between them and ourselves, and they have chosen these in preference to the life eternal.

'Originally men received the gospel message directly from the prophets and the first apostles, who preserved it true and inviolate and preached the faith in unity of belief. While the prophet is still alive, proclaiming his message and denouncing the sins of mankind in God's name, no man can plead ignorance as an excuse when he is called before God's judgment seat. The prophet makes atonement to God, and the people abide in righteousness and cleave for many years to His creed, law and authority. But later on, men rose up in revolt. They committed crimes, spurned prayer and gave free rein to their desires. Science was extinguished and scholars robbed of their learning. Hardly any of the sages survived, and the few who remained were treated with contempt by the untutored rabble. Wisdom was quenched and folly shone forth brightly.

'During these events, that generation passed away and another arose, which had no conception of the cause of true learning. So ignorance began to radiate and be diffused abroad, and knowledge to wane and be extinguished. The words of Holy Writ were falsified and their power perverted, and men abandoned the path of righteousness. People professed and interpreted the words of the sacred books in whatever sense they pleased. While clinging to the letter of the law, they abandoned its correct application. None the less, the word of truth endured, which even our adversaries received from the fountain head, and which the apostles preached. At the present time, we too accept those writings, but we oppose the fraud of the heretics, who only profess to accept the substance of Holy Writ, but are not worthy to establish the truth of it.'[1]

---

[1] This rather cryptic passage provides undeniable evidence of the Manichaean origins of much of the Barlaam and Josaphat romance. As Professor W. B. Henning has pointed out, the 'prophetology' in the corresponding passage of the Arabic version 'compellingly recalls authentic Manichaean writings'. ('Persian poetical manuscripts from the time of Rudaki, in A Locust's Leg. Studies in honour of S. H. Taqizadeh, London, 1962, p. 93.) Dr E. M. Boyce kindly drew my attention to an ancient Manichaean text from Central Asia, in which the idea of the inevitable corruption of earlier, inferior

23. Balahvar concluded by saying: 'I imagine that nobody has ever told all this to your father in his life, nor has anyone acted towards him with sincerity or made any real effort to make him understand these matters.'

Iodasaph answered: 'Why have the wise men taken no steps to approach him all this time?'

Balahvar replied: 'Because they knew they must wait for the right time and place before speaking their minds. Sometimes wise men have shrunk from reproaching people who were more amiable and receptive of justice and argument than your father is. It can happen that one man may be intimately associated with another for a very long time, and they may be on the most friendly terms with one another, and differ only on some questions of religion and philosophy. But even though the wise man may be very sorry for his deluded friend, yet he may never get round to revealing to him the secret of the wisdom which he holds.'

Iodasaph exclaimed: 'How can such a thing occur?'

---

religions after the death of their founder is explicitly stated. In this passage, Mani himself writes:

'The religion which I have devised is in ten respects superior and better compared with the other, earlier religions [e.g. Buddhism, Zoroastrianism and Christianity].

'Firstly: The earlier religions existed only in a single country and in a single language. My religion on the other hand is such that it will make its appearance in every country and in every tongue, and be taught in the furthest lands.

'Secondly: The earlier creeds continued in force only so long as their actual founders were there to direct them in person. But when their founders passed away, then their religious communities fell into confusion and became remiss in their precepts and works . . .

'But my religion, thanks to its good organization through the living scriptures, as well as through the agency of teachers, bishops, Elect and Hearers, and through wisdom and works, will last until the end of the world . . .'

(See F. C. Andreas and Walter Henning, 'Mitteliranische Manichaica aus Chinesisch-Turkestan, II', in *Sitzungsberichte der Preussischen Akademie der Wissenschaften*, Phil.-Hist. Klasse, Berlin, 1933, VII, pp. 4-5; also al-Biruni, *The Chronology of Ancient Nations*, trans. C. E. Sachau, London, 1879, p. 190.)

The general question of the Manichaean origins of the Barlaam romance is also discussed in D. M. Lang, *The Wisdom of Balahvar*, London, 1957, pp. 24-9.

BARLAAM AND JOSAPHAT

FABLE THE NINTH

The King and the Happy Poor Couple

Balahvar said: 'Here is a parable concerning a certain king who governed his realm with wisdom and sagacity, made great efforts to secure public tranquillity, and administered the temporal affairs of his kingdom as befits those monarchs who are inspired by love for their people. Now that king had a counsellor, a virtuous and upright man who eschewed all evil-doing, and constantly encouraged the king to adopt righteous and beneficent measures towards his subjects. Now this man was initiated into the rites of the true faith and had frequent meetings with wise people who had abandoned the life of this world. He was moreover a man of careful and sound judgment, and used to speak to the king with the utmost candour, though without revealing his personal secret to him. And so he remained a secret adherent of God's righteous cause.

'Now when this minister saw the king bowing down in front of idols and celebrating their solemn festivals, he was deeply grieved, like a man who grieves for his own son when the devil holds him in his clutches. Often he desired to discuss religion with him, and he consulted his friends about the problem. But they said: "You are the person most familiar with his intimate thoughts, and if you find an opportunity, then you might have a word with him. But be on your guard, for the devil is unsleeping in the cause of evil, and it would be a bad thing if Satan were to alienate the king's affections from you and incite him to persecute your associates."

'As the minister sorrowed greatly for the king's sake, he watched for a good moment to utter a word of warning to him. A long time went by like this, until one night the king said to his counsellor: "Come, let us go for a walk in the town, so that we may see how the people are faring!" In the course of their walk through the city, they came upon a large garbage mound.[1]

---

[1] This parable has its roots in the popular traditions of Baghdad in the time of the Caliph Harun al-Rashid (786-809), who was renowned for his habit of walking incognito round the city at night and observing the behaviour of his subjects. The episode of feasting, dancing and love-making in a giant rubbish heap has its parallel in the *Arabian Nights*, where the wife of an ensorcelled prince makes love to a loathsome negro in a cave dug out of a giant refuse mound. (See *The Book of the Thousand Nights and a Night*, trans. Sir Richard

And the king saw a ray of light, as of a fire, issuing forth. So the king and his counsellor turned aside to look at this. When they drew near, they discovered a man who had hollowed out a kind of cave inside the mound of refuse and was sitting within it together with his spouse. They were wearing ragged clothes, like those of beggars. As they gazed upon this sight, the sound of singing was heard coming forth. When they examined the interior of the cavern, they saw that the man was at table seated on a pile of manure, while the woman poured out wine for him, danced before him and flattered him with praises such as befit kings. She called him "My Lord", and he addressed her as "My Queen", and they both sang each other's praises and were gay and merry in their mutual affection.

'The monarch and his minister looked on for a long time and observed their behaviour attentively, watching how they passed their time in good cheer amid such squalid conditions. When the king and his counsellor left those people, they went away filled with amazement. And the king said to his companion: "Never have we found our life so desirable, nor have we enjoyed it with such relish as that poor wretch whom we have seen in the rubbish heap along with his wife. And I suppose that all their days are passed in the same fashion."

'The minister now took his chance to have a talk with the king, and said to him: "Do you not appreciate, O king, that the glory and dominion in which we ourselves revel are just as valueless and contemptible in the eyes of those who know the eternal glory and dominion which God will prepare for those who love Him? The gold-sculpted mansions which we build, the beauty of paintings and the splendour of our raiment—all these things are despised by those who see the temples of the life hereafter not made by hand, and celestial raiment invisible to the eye; and they consider these luxuries of ours just as worthless as we find the squalor in which those poor folk lead their lives. And the complacency which we feel in our exalted station is no less ridiculous than the self-esteem of those paupers, which we viewed with critical and amazed eyes."

F. Burton, I, pp. 71-73.) Sir Richard Burton adds a note to his translation of this passage, pointing out that some of the rubbish heaps which outlie Eastern cities, particularly those around Cairo, are over a hundred feet high.

'The king said to him: "Are there then wise men who are versed in such matters?"

'The other replied: "There are indeed men who serve God and have abandoned this world and spurned every aspect of temporal life; and they dwell now in the wilderness, in the mountains and in catacombs for the love of Christ. They have caught a glimpse of the life eternal and have fallen in love with it, after testing out this world and finding all its glory to be transitory."

'The king asked: "Now what is the nature of that eternal realm?"

'The counsellor replied: "The eternal realm is bliss not followed by wretchedness; it is joy not followed by sorrow; it is health not followed by sickness; it is royalty which has no end. It is tranquillity not pursued by fear, and life not interrupted by death; and it is a land of things imperishable, whose inhabitants receive their desire without any toil or anxiety."

'The king said: "Can any man be worthy to live there? How can a person gain entry to this place?"[1]

'The counsellor said to the king: "The gate of Christ is barred against no one who seeks to enter in thereby."

'The king said: "What road leads there?"

'The counsellor answered: "The service of the Holy Trinity, which gave birth to all created things, and renunciation of every cult but this."

'The king said: "What has prevented you up till now from telling me about this road?"

'The counsellor said: "It was not through any infidelity of my own that I deferred the matter until now, nor was I discouraged by any lack of perception on your part, because you are perfect in every respect. But the awe of your royal majesty held me back."

'The king said: "If what you have told me be true, we must lose no time in following it up with all possible speed and effort. If there be any doubt, then we must work hard until we discover what truth there is in it. But it was very wrong of you to keep this subject hidden from me, especially in view of the complete trust I place in you."

'The minister answered: "Is it now your command that I

---

[1] Here the copyist has added a note: 'Christ have mercy on David, Amen.'

should regularly inform and remind you about this matter from time to time?"

'The king said: "Not from time to time, but incessantly! You and I must keep watch vigilantly day and night, for this is a matter of marvellous import. It would be shameful to allow such a treasure to perish through neglect; rather must it be tended with fervent zeal." '

And the holy Balahvar added: 'We have heard tell that after this, the king and his counsellor departed in peace from out of this earthly life.'

24. Iodasaph exclaimed: 'No longer has my mind any love whatever for this world, nor will I occupy myself any more with its affairs. But I long for the life eternal, and intend to cleave to you and follow you wherever you go, and endure the austerity of your way of life.'

FABLE THE TENTH

The Rich Youth and the Poor Maiden

The holy Balahvar said: 'If you do this, you will be like that rich bridegroom who received a poor man as his father-in-law.— For we have heard that once there lived a certain youth, son of a wealthy man. And his father arranged for him to wed a beautiful and rich maiden from among his own kinsfolk. But the young man refused to marry her, and arose and fled away from his father's face. In the course of his wanderings, he caught sight of a poor man's daughter, dressed in humble garments, sitting on the threshold of her cottage. While busily engaged on her handwork, she was offering up thanks and praises to God.

'The youth asked her: "Who are you, O maiden, and for what blessings are you thanking God?"

'But she said to him: "Do not you know that a little medicine saves a person from many forms of illness? Likewise, to be thankful for small mercies can win us greater blessings. As for me, I am the daughter of a poor old man."

'Then the youth called out to her old father. When he came out, the young man said to him: "Are you willing to give this daughter of yours to be my wife?"

'The old man replied: "A poor man's daughter is not fit to be your bride, for you are a rich man's son."

'The young man said: "I have perceived the wisdom and intelligence of your daughter, and will be overjoyed to take her as my wife. Behold, a daughter born of rich parents was betrothed to me, but I refused her. Now pray fulfil my request, and you will find me an excellent son-in-law, if the Lord so will it."

'The old man said to him: "However much you long to wed my daughter, you will never be able to take her home to your father's mansion."

'The youth answered him: "Then I shall settle down here among you, and adopt your manner of life."

"However, that old man possessed a great store of hidden wealth. And the youth entered the old man's house, stripped off his apparel, and put on poor men's raiment. Then the old man began to test him and weigh up his understanding. When he had found him to be wise and intelligent in every respect, the old man realized that it was no frivolous infatuation that had led the youth to embrace a life of poverty. So he took him by the hand and led him into his treasure house and showed him all his riches and the beauties of that place, which were such that the young man had never seen in his entire life. And he said to him: "Son, all this is yours!" And thenceforward that youth enjoyed himself there in gaiety and delight.'

25. Iodasaph said: 'I pray to Christ the Son of God that this parable may be applied to me. But I understand you to state that the old man tested that youth's understanding. How then do you propose to test my intelligence?'

Balahvar said: 'Fear God, and follow His command all the days of your life, and renounce all the sins of the world. God will not rob you of the reward of your efforts, neither will He assist any dubious enterprise. You must grow in strength, for God does not test a man beyond his capacity. Remember the Lord day by day, perfect your mind, and tackle all problems after careful reflection. Do not be content to adopt the first inspiration which comes your way simply because it is an agreeable one, nor shrink from the revelation of truth because it seems severe. Test out the fibre of your heart, that you may not succumb to doubt. Do not hasten to blurt out the first ideas which enter your head, until you have had time to test them out calmly and cautiously. Let not your mind incline towards wilfulness and passion, lest you lose faith in virtue and succumb to evil. Now I shall pray for your sake to the Father of Our Lord Jesus Christ, Creator of the heavens and the earth, the Being who is firm and unshakeable and of the same substance as the Holy Ghost, having no end, terrible and gracious, mighty and merciful, invisible and inexpressible, benevolent in His royalty, omniscient and not oblivious, and powerful above all other beings. He is without fault, and whatever He promises He carries out without deceit. He cherishes all and abandons none. Before Him tremble all created beings, who kneel with bended neck before the terrible presence of His divine majesty. I shall beseech God that He will cleanse you, to be a true mentor of righteousness, an exemplary model of reverence, a giver of sight to the blind, of hearing to the deaf, a reproach to the idle and a foe of the world, a lover of the saints and detester of sinful passions, until He causes you to attain with us to that abode which Christ has promised us with His truth-giving lips—to that unimaginable kingdom of His, of which no man has heard, invisible to our eyes; for great is the trust which we place in Christ's mercies, great our dread of the torments which He metes out to sinners. Our eyes are directed towards Him, and our necks bowed down before Him.'

The holy Balahvar's words affected Iodasaph deeply, and his heart welled over and he began to sob. Then he said to Balahvar: 'How old are you, holy Father?'

He answered: 'I am twelve years old!'

Iodasaph exclaimed: 'How can you tell me this? For I can see that you are an elderly man, and you must surely be about sixty years of age.'

Balahvar replied: 'Counting from the time I was born, I am sixty years old, but you are asking me about the span of my life. Now life denotes the condition of being alive, and there is no live existence outside the faith of Christ and His works. And in these I had no part until twelve years ago.'

Iodasaph said to him: 'How can you treat a person who eats and drinks and walks about as a dead man?'

Balahvar replied: 'It is because such a one partakes of the nature of the dead by his blindness, deafness and weakness, his inability to help himself or to appreciate the good things of God, such as health and the aspiration towards virtuous ways.[1] If in his conduct a man chooses to belong to the dead, he must expect to share their name into the bargain.'

Iodasaph said: 'If you do not consider your previous life to be any life at all, it follows that you cannot consider the death which lies before us to be death either, nor regard it as an evil.'

Balahvar said: 'Does not the risk that I incur in visiting you provide evidence of this? For I am well aware of your father's hostility towards me. But I regard death in no sense as an evil, but rather as life eternal.'

26. Iodasaph said: Tell me a parable about this nation of ours, and its steadfast attachment to idols.'

FABLE THE ELEVENTH

The Fowler and the Nightingale

Balahvar answered: 'Those who believe in idols are like a certain man who caught a nightingale, as our fabulist relates, and wanted to kill her. But that nightingale was endowed with the power of speech, and she said: "Why do you wish to kill me? For you cannot satisfy your appetite on me! But if you will release me, I will teach you three precepts, and these will be of greater value to you than all your possessions if only you will abide by them."

'So she persuaded the man to let her go, on condition that she told him those precepts. When he had released her, the nightingale said: "These are my precepts:

> Do not seek for the unattainable;
> Do not regret what is past;
> Never believe what passes belief."

'After he had let her go, the nightingale wanted to test that man,to see whether he had profited by her precepts. So she said

---

[1] Ilia Abuladze's edition, p. 57, l. 7, has *sikharulit'a* 'by joy'. S. Qaukhchishvili (*Bizantiuri literaturis istoria*, p. 216) reads *siquarulit'a* 'by love', but points out that the correct reading must be *siqruit'a* 'by deafness', to fit in with the context, as well as with the Arabic version, which refers to 'blindness, deafness, etc.'

PLATE III

The Nightingale and the bird catcher

The Baptism of Iodasaph

King Abenes and the Ascetics

PLATE IV

Theudas acknowledging Christ

Iodasaph in the desert

to him: "If only you had known what a treasure has slipped through your hands! For in my crop there is a pearl as big as an ostrich egg."

'When the man heard this statement, he wept with mortification at having released her, and wanted to catch her again. So he said to her: "Come into my home, and I will look after you well and send you on your way with honour."

'But the nightingale answered him: "O ignorant fellow, you caught me and could not hold me; I taught you, and you could not take in the lesson I gave you in exchange for my freedom. What about those maxims I taught you? Here you are now, ruing having set me free, which is something that is past; you are seeking for the unattainable, namely to recapture me; and believing something which passes belief, namely that I have in my crop a pearl bigger than my own self. Fancy not realizing that my entire body is not the size of an ostrich egg!"—From then onwards that man took to heart those words of hers and profited by them.

'Equally ridiculous is the faith which men place in idols: for these are things made by human hands, and yet men declare: "These are our creators!" They safeguard these gods of theirs from being stolen by thieves, yet they say: "These are our guardians from evil!" They squander their wealth on them, saying: "These are our foster-parents!" They seek to receive from them that which they can never find, and believe them to possess qualities which can never be theirs.'

Iodasaph said: 'This parable truly conveys the nature of idols, which are wholly loathsome to me. I have no faith in them, and your speech has aroused my hatred of them to greater intensity. But what is the faith to which you call me? What is this creed which you yourself have chosen to follow?'

Balahvar said to him: 'Here is the basis of this creed which I have chosen.—There exists one Father, Son and Holy Spirit, a Trinity of three persons and one divine essence, and not a multiplicity of godheads. God alone is King, and all things beside Him form His kingdom; He alone is the Creator, all others are created; He alone is timeless, all others are temporal; He alone is strong, all others are weak; He alone is high, all others are low. He is ever vigilant, omniscient and omnipotent to do and achieve all things which He wills. "All things were made by Him; and without Him was not any thing made that was made."[1] Untouched by the passage of time and unchanging from one place to another, all space is filled with His presence, gracious and merciful as He is, and full of love and justice towards men. And He has prepared abodes of joy for those that obey Him, and abodes of torment for the disobedient. Now may He, made manifest in the Trinity and worshipped in one essence, make you a seeker out of His will, that you may live through the power of His undivided nature. If you observe His commands, then you shall attain as is fitting to knowledge of His truth.'

27. Iodasaph asked: 'What kind of deeds are pleasing to God?'
Balahvar said to him: 'It is God's will that whatever you would desire for yourself, you should do unto your neighbour; and whatever you would not desire, you should not do unto another. Observe Christ's teachings and abide in prayer[2] [and supplication day and night, and you shall have His Cross for the vanquishing of your foes; for it is thereby that He has saved me from the pains of death.'

Iodasaph said to Balahvar: 'By observing the commandments, shall a man fulfil God's will?'

Balahvar said: 'Yes, he shall fulfil it indeed.'

—'Seeing that there are such excellent things in the world, why then have you rejected them?'

Balahvar said: 'Two things impel us to do this.—First, the fact that the supreme blessings of God cannot be compared with the trifling joys of the realms here below. And whoever shall strive, he shall receive the greater honour. A friend may well come to feel no small jealousy towards his fellow; after all, people who pay merely what tax is due are not on the same footing as those who give free bounty.

'The second is this: Beware of indulging in proffered delights, whereby one is involved in unseemly doings and incurs condemnation. But if you shun them, you will receive peace and comfort abounding. If someone leads his herds too near the corn-

---

[1] John, i. 3.
[2] Two folios are missing here from the Jerusalem manuscript of *Balavariani*. The gap has been filled by inserting the corresponding passage from the shorter recension of the Georgian text. (*The Wisdom of Balahvar*, trans. D. M. Lang, London, 1957, pp. 90-1.)

fields, he cannot feel secure, for if he dozes off or becomes careless, the cattle will trample on the crops. It is only when he has driven them home away from the crops that he can sleep and rest with a quiet mind.'

Iodasaph said: 'What you are telling me is entirely true. Add however a further discourse to make me grow in hate and detestation of this world.'

Balahvar said: 'Let this be quite clear to you, that revulsion from the world reconciles man with God. Since this life is short, and the days and nights soon flow away, let us now make an effort to abandon the world voluntarily, for willy-nilly, we are fated to leave it sooner or later. Even if our life be long drawn out, death is yet in store for us. Then all a man's possessions shall be scattered abroad and his lofty buildings ruined; and his name shall become unknown and his memory wiped out; and his body shall shrink away; for they shall carry him forth naked from his dwelling-place and consign him to the dark cavern and lay him down by himself in a strange place, forsaken in his wretched state by those that hate him. And everyone shall abandon and revile him, even his wife, brethren and children.'

28. At this, Iodasaph wept and said: 'Your words have pierced my heart! Now speak to me about salvation.'

Balahvar continued: 'Even I, O king's son, was greatly fond of this world and absorbed in its delights. But when I had taken thought and seen the vicissitudes][1] which beset those that dwell in it, and how all men must leave it at last, I realized that no one can endure therein permanently, neither the great man by his greatness, nor the strong man by his strength, nor the clever man by his cleverness, nor the wise man by his wisdom. I perceived that I am a mere mortal just as they, and must pass away just as they passed away, and my place will be taken by others just as theirs were. Since I am no greater than the great nor stronger than the strong, whatever has befallen them must befall me also. I learnt that everything which has been amassed must be scattered and every treasure cast to the winds. Only the fear of God and the learning of His commands can deliver us

---

[1] At this point we resume our translation from the Jerusalem manuscript, in the edition of Professor Ilia Abuladze.

from eternal condemnation.[1] This is the only conduct which can relieve our penitence at death's approach. When I had realized all this, I sought out for myself some better way of life, and treated my own desires with utter contempt as being a source of sin, even though I found this very difficult. I renounced my ambitions and bridled them with the bridle of God's fear, that they might not lead me astray and plunge me into the distractions of this vain world.

'And then I heard the voice of our Lord God, who has taught us in divinely inspired books, saying: "I have created this world and all its semblance as something transitory. Take up now provisions for the way, for you shall depart into a strange land. Since you shall certainly pass over into the world beyond, take heed that you carry nothing out of this world besides what you need on the road until you arrive there. I have prepared an eternal mansion, in which are two habitations. One of these abodes is supplied with everything unspeakably good and with all manner of delights; I have filled it with my bounty and benevolence, so that it may be a place of reward for those who have loved me and placed their faith in the voice of my prophets and observed my commandments, and therein they shall enjoy bliss imperishably and death shall have no hold over them, seeing that they are in a place where neither fear nor worldly care exists. But the second abode is full of tortures, suffering and hardship, with shame and envy, boiling over with wrath and anger, with which I shall mete out retribution on all those who hate me and have despitefully used my prophets, forgotten my commandments and turned their ears away from my words of warning."

'When I heard God's voice, I realized that His words are just and His commandments true. So I took up provisions for the way, so that I might attain to the abode of peace and bounty by good deeds and obeying the commandments. And now I flee from that fearsome abode by avoiding all acts of disobedience, although neither I nor any other of the great ones of the world are capable of attaining to that holy estate to bring about which Christ laid down His life upon the Cross, and in quest of which we must follow His example; for many are my sins and I live in

[1] Here the copyist has added a note: 'Deliver, O Lord, the soul of David from eternal condemnation.'

great dread lest the Holy Virgin Mary and all God's saints withhold their intercession from me.'[1]

Iodasaph asked him: 'How is it possible to attain to those good things of which you speak?'

Balahvar replied: 'A man must quit the world and all preoccupation with it, taking with him only what is absolutely essential. Beware of the last judgment and stand fast in God's teaching. Affirm nothing before you have tried it out; for a little righteousness unmixed with sin is better than great virtues in which sin is also mingled. It is likewise better to speak only in moderation rather than over-eloquently, because in all wordiness there is an element of falsehood. It is a wise man's duty to instruct his own self, just as a good pastor instructs his people, diligently managing their affairs by his efforts, shielding them from harmful influences, and then showing his esteem for those that are obedient. It likewise behoves a wise man to examine himself in all his deeds and impulses, and then mete out justice to his own self, after judging whether he has acted so as to merit reward or retribution. If his deeds are good, he may be pleased and gratified with himself; if he finds his own conduct worthless, then he must chasten himself with repentance. Similarly, an intelligent man must keep watch on his own impulses and perfect his reason, and likewise use this reason of his to drive out evil. He must criticize himself and have enough sense to mistrust his own mental powers, lest his character become tainted with conceit. For God hates conceit and loves wisdom and humility, because it is through wisdom that man attains to virtue by God's ordinance, and through ignorance that many souls perish. The chief source of fortitude is the fear of the Lord and walking in His ways. Likewise the chief of all evils is the pursuit of lusts and subservience to desires. When you are beset by thoughts which your brain is incapable of fathoming, do not struggle vainly to find a solution to them, for this may only unsettle your wits and befuddle your intellect. Try to be more relaxed, thus enabling your intellect to grasp and your soul to distinguish the supreme good. When confronted with some knotty problem, do not react with resentment or declare that it cannot be solved.

---

[1] Note by the copyist in the Manuscript: 'O Christ, have mercy on Chita, Amen.'

Rather should you attempt to bring it to the most successful outcome.

'Know this too, that no single mortal can absorb all forms of knowledge. A wise man should not despise a mere smattering of knowledge, especially when he is unable to master the subject completely. Even the eyes of a sage cannot absorb the full brilliance of the sun. The few rays of the sun which he can stand are quite sufficient to guide him on his daily round. The excess radiance which he is unable to endure serves only to dazzle him and obstruct his vision. What man can eat every dish simultaneously, and swallow every drink which he may see and fancy? Nobody is capable of digesting more than a small part of them! But even without consuming vast quantities of every foodstuff, a person can appreciate delicate flavours and satisfy his appetite with meals of moderate size.

'Wisdom and virtue are of more importance and greater and more worthy than mere food, provided that a man's eye is capable of focusing on them, his heart of absorbing them and his mind of profiting by them. This kind of excellence is harder of attainment than that which we have expounded through the metaphors of the sun and of food. God has ordained that wise men shall possess differing degrees of wisdom. But there is nothing to prevent each man from making use of wisdom according to his individual capacity. His failure to grasp the things he knows not does not hinder him from utilizing what little he does know.'

29. Iodasaph asked: 'How should a man like myself set about ferreting out the truth from the doctrines of heretical sects?'

Balahvar replied: 'By collecting together all the issues of doctrine on which the conflicting sects are agreed, in so far as they profess belief in our Lord Jesus, and preserving those articles of faith over which they are not at variance. A selection should then be made, according to the following principle: firstly, by studying books and comparing examples, verification by the intelligence and confirmation by practical experience; then by rejecting what is dubious and not relying on human opinions. A man who persists in his purpose, wherever it may lead him, is in a better posture to cope with whatever situations he may encounter than one who arbitrarily adopts a position which conflicts with the dictates of his conviction and knowledge; for he who stands on firm ground rests on the basis of truth and steers clear of error. But one who persists in wrong-headed deeds which conflict with his knowledge and conviction will undoubtedly go astray. Such is the situation in this world, for the sum of human knowledge is greater than the sum of human ignorance. A man must do what good he knows how, and avoid what evils he can recognize as such. Let him be zealous and loyal to God by his behaviour both in secret and in public. When he shall do these things, God will open the gate of wisdom and reveal His will to him, and he shall easily undo the devil's most dangerous snares.'

Iodasaph asked: 'How is a man to strive with zeal and loyalty in the faith?'

Balahvar replied: 'His aim should be to put aside from his heart the summons of desire and the distractions of lust, and devote his prime faculties to the affairs of the faith and true endurance and religion. When he does this, he shall win the fruit of knowledge and God will wipe out his sorrow and doubt.'

Iodasaph asked: 'On such occasions must one be prepared for a long wait?'

Balahvar said to him: 'That is so. However, there is no need to mistrust the first principles which a man learns. Let him train his reason to receive them through the medium of authentic teaching, representation and interpretation.'

Iodasaph said: 'What would you say if someone were to analyze a number of similar, parallel cases with all the labour and mental effort at his disposal, and still failed to distinguish truth from delusion? Will his perseverance be deemed sufficient, so that he may desist from his enquiry, with the prospect that God will reward him as highly as his fellows?'

Balahvar answered him: 'Enquiry into every matter is a good thing. If a man cannot discover something which is past, he should carefully consider and persistently ferret out the present state of the business, until its nature is unveiled by true evidence, or revealed to him through long time spent in that enquiry. Let him not give up his trust in God, but wait rather for a revelation to come from God Himself. Meanwhile let him not be deterred from continuing his researches steadfastly, however much the mind may boggle at a problem at the first encounter. Provided that he applies himself with patience, pursues his enquiries steadfastly and with a good hope, and investigates the history of the business, his current doubts will be dissipated. Then he will be free from all doubt and mystery, until he can perceive the gate through which to enter in, and stray no more from the way of truth. A sage should not lose heart at his failure to gain admission through one door of knowledge, but should then proceed to make trial of a second. Nor should ignorance of one single aspect of a matter cause a man to abandon the subject altogether. No man can attain knowledge of everything he seeks; nor is all knowledge necessarily profitable, nor all ignorance invariably harmful.'

'Now the devil's most reliable traps are the two following devices: the first is to inspire the mind of a wise man with the idea that wisdom and reason have abandoned him, that there is no more profit for him in learning—in fact, that ignorance is no handicap to a man at all. The devil shows him a man revelling in the delights of the world, and says to his victim: "Behold now the honourable estate and the glory to which that other man has attained without any scholarly learning at all! Why do you torment yourself and undergo such pain? Drink, eat and be merry, for tomorrow you die![1] There is no point in going out to meet death of your own accord, before it first descends on you in its own good time."—With this and similar barbs the devil pierces his heart through, and deters him from the pursuit of learning. He causes the man to glimpse vistas of opulence, so that he may be pursued by the habits of self-indulgence and haunted by temptations.

'But if the devil cannot prevail by this method, and observes that his victim has developed powers of resistance, he despatches from his quiver a second arrow, tipped with red-hot steel. When he realizes that his wiles are detected on the left flank, he directs his assault to the right flank of his victim's armour and embarks on a plan of attack for which he is unprepared. And the evil one unleashes upon that man the spirit of disgust, until he makes him loathe every aspect of his life's work and regard himself as contemptible, despicable and foolish. The wise man curses his own learning and reviles and ridicules his friends and mentors.

---

[1] Isaiah, xxii. 13.

Then the devil says to him: "You will never win success in this career of yours nor bring it to fulfilment, nor be strong enough to endure the weight of its discipline. So why are you tormenting yourself and toiling away after an ambition which you can never attain?" Then the evil one adds: "If you aspire to perfect your virtue and not betray God, you must fast for forty days and go about constantly in ashes, sackcloth and tears."—Such obstacles as these the devil places in people's way, to make them lose heart and despair, and then succumb. Or else he exalts them beyond measure, and then casts them down to earth again.

'By inflicting such misery he clouds a man's understanding, so that he can no longer judge accurately nor withstand the impact of temptation. Many mortals have been wounded and slaughtered by these two arrows, because the soul is quick to relish fruit which the reason cannot digest. For reason and desire are at enmity with one another, and are battling constantly for control of the soul. Desire is a kind friend to the soul, but reason is its severe mentor. For desire relieves all the soul's troubles, lulls it with tempting allurements, and renders it oblivious to worry and fear. But reason invokes hardship and bids one live in misery; it banishes passions and reproves sin, showing how indulgence in the delights of this life opens the broad way to eternal torment in the future. It makes a man rue his past sloth, and condemns his future idleness. The soul is greatly inclined to follow the dictates of desire, but there are two methods of resisting these temptations which desire assembles. Firstly, abstain from all vanities, secondly, strive steadfastly to attain what little virtue you are capable of grasping, as well as aspiring continually for the good qualities which transcend your reach. Observe this lesson, learn it well, and arm yourself with it; and may Our Lord God the Father of Our Lord Jesus Christ be your help in all your doings, for there exists no strength nor power except that which proceeds from Jesus Christ, to whom belongs glory together with the Father and the Holy Spirit now and always and for ever and ever, Amen.'

30. Iodasaph said: 'I have listened to your discourse and glorification of God. Add now an even clearer description, so that I may see God's image as if with my own eyes.'

Balahvar said: 'Inexpressible is the likeness of the Godhead, and the mind cannot fathom its nature. Neither are any tongues capable of worthily praising Him. Knowledge of Him is inaccessible to created beings, apart from what He has revealed by the mouth of the prophets. No one has the right to speak of Him to mankind, except for Him who was born of the Godhead prior to eternity, namely Our Lord Jesus Christ, who proceeded from God the Father. It was Our Lord who proclaimed Him to us, for His likeness is invisible to the eyes; and the prophets testified concerning Him and convinced mankind of His authority by means of signs and miracles, which He gave them to perform by power such as was vouchsafed to no one else. For He exercises His power universally in the heavens and on earth, in the seas and in all the depths.'

Iodasaph said: 'What is the evidence for the knowledge of God?'

Balahvar replied: 'The sky and the earth and all that dwell therein, things spiritual and creatures endowed with flesh. If you see some vessel which has been fashioned, even though you may not have seen its maker, you believe all the same that it had someone to make it. Similarly, in the case of a building, even if you cannot see the man who built it, your reason still tells you that it has a builder. As for me, when I looked attentively at my own anatomy, I was amazed; and although I could not see my Maker, I know that He gave me birth according to His will and shaped me in accordance with His design, quite apart from my own choice. If I had been my own creator, I should have made myself superior in physical beauty and bodily perfection to all other created beings; but He who created me according to His own design made me greater than many of His creatures and less than others. Later I also realized that He will bear me away out of this life without asking my consent. And I see that events will befall me from unknown quarters, without my having knowledge of the length of my life-span, nor what evil may overtake me in its course. And I perceive that all men are in like case to myself: for no man can either add to or take away from his stature,[1] or replace a worn-out body, nor can he fasten on afresh any limb which may have fallen away. Kings have not been able to perform this by their sovereignty nor wise men by

---

[1] Matthew, vi. 27; Luke, xii. 25.

their wisdom; neither have clever men succeeded in this by their cleverness, nor strong men by the strength.

'Then again, we observe the drawing in of evening following the day, the dawning of day following the night, and the revolution of the spheres. Thereby we know that all those created beings have a Creator, being of a different nature from them. If He did resemble them, He would be just like one of them, and would be governed by the same forces which govern each one of them. Everything which we see has been created, and the creation of those things bears witness to this fact; some of them have come into existence by conjunction, and others by reproduction; some are formed by separation and others by definition, abbreviation and extension within the time scale, as well as by stirring into motion or else by inducing stability. He created them from nothing and fashioned them without any previous model. He said: "Be!" And they were. Whenever He so desires, all will pass away. And again, He can restore them to being, just as they were previously. His command is sharper than a double-edged sword[1] and swifter than a lightning flash. He summons them and they draw near; He scatters them and they are dispersed; and again He brings them into order and they resume their shape. And blessed and glorious and exalted exceedingly is the name of the Holy Trinity for evermore.'

31. Iodasaph exclaimed: 'All that you have told me about the origin of created things, namely that apart from God nothing came into being, this I have taken in; for you have convinced me by means of true testimony and lucid instances. Yet how do you know whether there is any resurrection after death, and any repayment for good works and for evil?'

Balahvar answered: 'There are two things which make this manifest. Firstly, there is a great difference between the way in which the devout and the unbelievers live in this world, since we see many unbelievers quitting this earth in luxury, honour and tranquillity, whereas many of the devout pass into the world beyond in poor, despised and straitened circumstances. Thereby one knows that the just Judge has forborne from glorifying His devout ones in this world in terms of luxury and

---

[1] Hebrews, iv. 12.

honours, simply in order to prepare for them eternal honour in the world hereafter, although the disobedience of mortals can in no way harm God, nor their obedience further His designs.

'In the second place, this is made evident through the preaching of the apostles, for they uttered glad tidings to mankind of eternal reward for the faithful, and gave warning of eternal torments for the disobedient. I accept their testimony on these secret mysteries, because they displayed signs and miracles with powers which no human being could command without the agency of the one and only Godhead.'

32. Iodasaph said: 'Tell me now, since the apostles were men of ordinary human stuff and of like character to other men, how can you distinguish them from their fellow beings, and how do you know whether they are telling the truth?'

Balahvar told him: 'I know the truth of their words from the fact that they have renounced this world and those that dwell therein, and have resisted its demands and exhorted men to conform to righteous ideals on all occasions — in wrath and in tranquillity, in poverty and in wealth, in lowliness and in exaltation, and in seeking asylum from the path of tyrants. They urge us to distinguish between the honourable and the dishonourable, to endure spiteful treatment patiently, to abandon self-will and submit to privation, to abide by the commandments and submit to the tribunal of justice whenever a man is called upon to face it. These burdens of theirs are exceedingly heavy to bear, and their yoke is tight and irksome. Now if they had been false prophets of God and liars, they would not have led men along such narrow and difficult paths. They would sooner have offered them vistas to delight human nature, and shown them a broad path and a spacious gate such as would please the eyes and captivate the heart. They would have pandered to their enjoyments and lusts and encouraged them in gracious living and won over men's hearts by this kind of approach. They would not have alarmed people by their prayers, fasting and endurance in travail, and by treating both rich and poor on a footing of equality. That is how we know that they speak true, and their deeds also testify to this, for no ordinary mortals could manifest such marvels and signs as they!'

Iodasaph asked: 'If any man were to arise and falsely declare himself an apostle of God and set himself up as a preacher, how can one detect whether he is telling the truth or a pack of lies?'

Balahvar replied: 'His works will declare his hidden secrets and his preaching will be discredited by his behaviour. For such impostors preach long-suffering and are themselves incapable of endurance; they teach virtue and practise vice; nor are they capable of performing any miracle which surpasses the powers of man. If however any true prophet departs this life, among his papers will be found a message specifying the successor who is coming to continue his ministry.'

Iodasaph enquired: 'Now supposing there happened to be a certain man versed in ancient writings and records of events gone by, and that he had learnt from these that such a man was expected to come; supposing furthermore that he discovered the names of the dead prophet and the one who was to come, and himself posed as the appointed successor — how is such an impostor to be found out, and his trickery exposed?'

The holy Balahvar said: 'The word of God is invincible, His light unquenchable, His truth inextinguishable. For God sends no prophet among a given generation other than one who is prominent among the people. Even prior to his mission, that man must be outstanding for his holiness, truth, calmness, physical purity and love of peace. He will not be wrathful, avaricious nor haughty; nor will he embark irresponsibly on any unrighteous course. When God sends such a man out to preach, He imparts to him strength in deed and in word. If previously he was halting in speech, God grants him the gift of eloquence, enabling him to utter glad tidings, to reprove, and to gain knowledge of things not revealed to ordinary men. Everything he does he performs with grace and even his hidden doings testify about him. No man can prevail against truth through falsehood, even if his false character has not been previously detected by the people, or some deed of his served to unmask his imposture. Again, justice cannot be established by lies, nor can falsehood produce and bring about any good thing.'

33. Balahvar's visits to the king's son became frequent. He kept on instructing and admonishing Iodasaph, until his retainers became astonished and amazed at Balahvar's untimely visitations.

Now the king had appointed as his son's servant and governor a certain loyal man in whom he had every confidence, whose name was Zadan. When Zadan got to know about Balahvar, he had a private word with the prince and said to him: 'You are aware of the position I hold in the king's service and my responsibility for you. Your father would not have appointed me to serve you, had he not trusted me completely. I am extremely surprised at the conduct of this individual who comes to see you all the time. I am afraid that he may belong to the sect which your father detests and has banned from the kingdom. Now if he purposes to do some good thing for you and you have no objection to your father's knowing, I had better inform the king, because we are very worried and disturbed about this matter. But if he is discussing some mystery with you, which you are unwilling for the king to learn of, then do one of three things for my sake: either having nothing further to do with him, and I will conceal what has occurred up to now; alternatively, you could refrain from anger and absolve us from blame, while letting us approach the king ourselves, meanwhile preparing a suitable explanation regarding this man and getting ready to present your own excuses; or finally, you can vent your wrath upon us by public disgrace and dismissal, and arrange for your father to give you other servants instead of us.'

The king's son answered Zadan and said: 'The first step I propose to take regarding you, Zadan, is to conceal you in this room, so that you can listen to our conversation. Afterwards I will tell you what I have decided to do.'

So the prince seated Zadan behind the curtain when Balahvar was due to visit him. They began to converse with one another, and Iodasaph made enquiry concerning the passing world. Then Balahvar according to his wont began to discourse on the vanity of the world and the glory of eternity and said: 'Those who seek after pleasure ought to choose eternal bliss in preference to this life which so swiftly passes by! Why is it that people addicted to this world's delights fail to realise that unless a thing is durable, it is not worth having at all? How can they fail to appreciate the superiority of those eternal blessings, compared with all this trifling, contemptible and swiftly perishing enjoyment? No one but a fool will immerse himself in love for this world, and no one but a deluded wretch will stray from the path towards life eternal. How can the business of amassing wealth make people other than wretched? For they are engaged in a contest for transitory riches which they know beyond any doubt must soon slip out of their hands. They know that every momentary pleasure changes after an instant from novelty to tedium! And yet they fail to deposit their treasures in the world eternal, where they are stored free from corruption! What worldly affair is worthy of praise, and what treasures of this earth can last without rotting away? What mortals are more pitiful than those who seek after wealth and are drunk with greed for riches, seeing that the more valuables they accumulate here below, the more misery will be added to their lot in heaven. The more honour they win here below, the more they will be put to shame and kept apart from God there above.'—And much similar converse and discussion they held together.

34. When Balahvar had left, Iodasaph wanted to test Zadan, to see whether he had been edified by Balahvar's words. So he said to him: 'Do you not hear what this liar and charlatan is telling me? He is trying to pervert me and spoil my enjoyment of this life, and inciting me to oppose the king!'

Zadan said to him: 'You have no need to resort to a ruse with me, O king's son, nor have you anything to be ashamed of, for this discourse is singular and luminous. In earlier times we too have listened to this doctrine and recognized its sweetness and the excellence of those who put it into practice. But since the time when the king persecuted and banned the Christian faith, we have no more been allowed to hear such tidings, for fear that our hearts might receive and cherish this doctrine. We realize that it was ignorance which made us turn our back on it, and give our preference to this life which passes away in an instant. As for you, O king's son, if you find the Christian faith pleasing and have chosen it for yourself, and are prepared to submit to its rigour, combined with the king's wrath, the people's hostility, and the austerities of its adepts—then be joyful through Christ in celestial glory and life eternal! I, however, am inhibited by my love for the passing world and awe before your father, although I do not deny the merits of this cause, nor would I oppose anyone who embraced it. But now please counsel me how to avoid incurring your father's anger, seeing that I have so far concealed this affair from him!'

Iodasaph said to Zadan: 'Was it not for your own benefit that I let you listen to this conversation of ours, in order that you might receive the message of salvation, which is life for the spirit? I could think of no greater reward for your loyalty and affection than to make you realize to what end you have been created, and help you to appreciate your own best interests. However, your response has not measured up to the hope I placed in you! As for the concealment of this matter, be this as you wish. It is not for my own sake that I fear the king's wrath, but for that of the king himself, for he takes this business greatly to heart. By telling him, you would only cause him worry and incite him to persecute the true believers. By keeping this matter secret, you will be performing an act of loyalty towards His Majesty, for you will spare his mind from grief and not be a harbinger of gloom, robbing him of hope in his son. For my part, I absolve you of all blame.'

35. Now Balahvar wanted to depart to his own abode, and came to take leave of the king's son. But Iodasaph was very sad and could not bear to be separated from him, and said to him: 'I cannot endure to exist without you, nor can I suffer you to depart. Rather let me go away with you, and we will dwell together in company with your comrades!'

FABLE THE TWELFTH

The Tame Gazelle

Balahvar said to him: 'Listen now, O king's son, to a parable which I propose to tell you. For I have heard that once there lived a certain man of rich and noble family, who had a little son. And for that child he reared the fawn of a gazelle. Now the boy became greatly attached to the fawn, to such an extent that he could not bear to be parted from it for a moment. But when the fawn grew up, her native instincts asserted themselves and she longed to run wild in the country. So one day she went out and caught sight of a herd of gazelles and joined their company. At first they shunned her because of her tameness, then they sniffed and smelt at one another. After this, she would sally forth from time to time, whenever her keepers relaxed their vigilance. The wild gazelles grew accustomed to her, and she would often tarry with them out in the open. When her guardians realized that she was reverting to the wild state, they felt that she might be overpowered by her original savage nature and return to them no more. The gazelles themselves then migrated to a more remote place, and the fawn too used to follow after them and return home even more tardily than at first. Then her keepers sent a man after her to spy out her doings and the place to which she was resorting. The man returned and reported that she was consorting with wild gazelles. Then the guardians mounted their steeds and set off on her trail. When they caught sight of her afar off, they gave chase to the wild gazelles, hunted them down and exterminated them; and they caught the tame fawn, carried her off and locked her up at home, and she was never allowed to venture forth again.

'I am afraid, O prince, that if you sally forth to join us, a like fate may befall me and my companions. We could not enjoy your company, nor could our hopes for the revival of the faith be fulfilled. Your own intimates might come to harm, and you would be prevented from achieving your own desire, which you might otherwise attain through striving in secret until you find the moment of real opportunity, if this be God's will. Your perseverance in this course of action will be more pleasing to God than for the king's wrath to be excited against those remaining brethren who would be doomed to annihilation in the event of your departure. We are not fleeing to escape ill-treatment and death at the king's hands, but because we do not want to give him a pretext to persecute my companions if we abduct you, nor do we wish to become a party to his godless deeds.'

36. Iodasaph asked: 'What kind of food do you subsist on in the wilderness?'

Balahvar replied: 'Herbs of the earth, watered by the dew, for the sake of which no one competes or quarrels with us. But if we are short of anything, some of our pious brethren dwelling in that region will supply us. And in our penurious state it seems to us only right and proper to accept their offerings.'

Iodasaph said: 'Then accept and take some articles of value, to save your companions from want!'

Balahvar retorted: 'How can you give any valuables to my companions, seeing that you are poorer even than they? For no poor man can give alms to a rich one, but only a rich one to a poor one, and the poorest of my companions is richer than you are! But I hope that if the Lord wills it, you too will become passing rich and that your fruits and your treasures may be multiplied. But then you will become miserly, and not so ready to distribute them to all and sundry!'

Iodasaph enquired: 'How comes it that the poorest of your companions is richer than I, after what you have been saying about their extreme poverty? How is it that I shall become miserly when my treasures are multiplied, whereas today I am lavish in giving?'

Balahvar replied: 'I do not speak of their poverty, but of the wealth which these brethren of yours confidently expect in the hereafter. They are perfectly content with their lot, and derive more delight and joy from renouncing pleasure than from all the wealth in the world. You also must aspire to such a way of life, for the rich man is he who has no truck with riches. But those who seek after treasure and wealth may be rich in material terms, but are poor in spirit. My comrades enjoy pre-eminence in happiness, for they are not men of this world, and have stored up treasures of good deeds in heaven, to which you yourself can as yet lay no claim. In this world they have comfort, joy and hope at the prospect of the good reward which will be meted out to those who depart this life after fulfilling the true doctrine of the orthodox faith. You also shall attain thither, if it be Christ's will, your fruit shall be multiplied, you shall set eyes on your brethren for whom you yearn, and you shall rejoice in one another. No longer will you squander those treasures which you will acquire there above. Then you will become really worthy to appreciate riches and store up precious things.

'As for the valuables which you have in mind to give to my companions—these would serve only to unsettle their minds. The aim of my mission is not to administer to them again the poison of this world, which they have fought and overcome by their exertions and by faith in Our Lord Jesus Christ, nor to revive their foe whom they have slain and the lusts which they have trampled underfoot. It is not good to set among them an enemy who would confuse them and remind them of the vain pleasures of this world, lest they falter and be plunged into poverty and ruin. As for this gold and silver, these carbuncles and pearls—what are they but different species of those same stones which exist in our own wilderness?'

Iodasaph asked: 'Whence do you procure your clothing?'

The holy Balahvar answered: 'This is our most difficult task of all, though we content ourselves for raiment with old bits of cloth gathered from refuse-heaps and sometimes garments woven from rushes and leaves, and we make do with one piece of clothing for a long period of time. When we change our clothes, we consider that our sufferings in this world are drawing to a close. If death comes upon our brother before his garment is worn out, the departed is laid to rest, now that the long-awaited day has arrived on which he placed his hope. But if the clothes wear out and the man remains alive, then they replace the garment in the way that I have just described to you. If we can find nothing more on the refuse-heaps and run out of raw materials for weaving together, in such dire necessity we accept gifts from the villages or from whatever source God sends them, whether it be from righteous men or from false.'

Iodasaph said: 'Accept from me some raiment for your companions, and share it out between them!'

Balahvar replied: 'This would constitute storing up goods for the future and is not lawful, as it is written in the Holy Gospel: "Do not be anxious about tomorrow, for tomorrow will be anxious about itself."[1] None of us changes his garment until it is completely worn out and does not cover up his flesh any longer. What is the point of making provision for some future day, when a man knows not whether he will reach that day or no?'

FABLE THE THIRTEENTH

The Costume of Enemies

37. Iodasaph asked: 'Then how did you come to dress yourself in your present fine raiment?'

---

[1] Matthew, vi. 34.

Balahvar said: 'I have put on this apparel in order to gain access to your presence, so that no one in your father's realm would be shocked by my appearance. Now this instance is like that of a person who has a kinsman in captivity, and wishes to deliver him from his foes. He cannot enter the enemies' country except by disguising his appearance and his costume, and so he adopts this stratagem in order to rescue his kinsman from the foes. By this method, he is enabled the more successfully to attain his objective.

'When I heard about you and learnt that you longed for righteousness and sought after the true Saviour, Jesus Christ, and yearned to hear the message of the Holy Gospel, then I realized that this mission would be profitable to my soul, and that I had found a fruitful ground for sowing. This is the path which leads to all men like you, whether they be high or low. But now I have delivered you from your foes by the power and intercession of Our Lord Jesus Christ and have rescued you from their clutches, for I have imparted to you the knowledge of God and the precepts of the apostles and Holy Fathers. And I have taught you the entire Christian creed and set you on your guard against this world and its snares, and the way in which it deludes men by its delights and lusts; and I have warned you against its wiles and exposed its shame to you, for it is a harlot and remains not constant in love for any man. So now I am departing to the scene of my tranquil existence, and there I shall strip off the guise of my enemies and don once more the likeness and garb of my brethren and companions. But if you had actually seen me dressed and attired like these companions of mine, I do not imagine that you would have been so eager to come away and join them!'

Then Iodasaph prayed him to show himself in the likeness of his companions. So Balahvar doffed his robes, exposing his entire skin drawn over his bones like the hide of a man dead through excessive fasting, stretched tightly over thin canes. He wore no clothes apart from a tattered hair apron hanging by a string from his navel and reaching down to his knees, as is the habit of ascetics. When Iodasaph saw this apron sewn from old rags hanging upon him, his heart welled up at the sight of this great symbol of godliness and armour of the sacred monastic habit which the holy Balahvar wore upon his person. Iodasaph began to weep and sob, and his bowels of compassion were moved for his sake. Like one who mourns at the prospect of his own death, so did Iodasaph weep bitterly at the prospect of Balahvar's departure.

38. And he said to him: 'If you will neither take me with you nor accept clothing or valuables for your companions, at least accept a garment for yourself!'

Balahvar replied: 'I have refused the gifts which you pressed on me for my companions, O prince, as they do not seek after such things. How then shall I take anything for my own use? How can I deny them possessions, but not deny myself? If it were right, I should collect things for them sooner than for myself.'

Iodasaph said: 'At least accept a new hair garment, and leave me yours, for I want to keep something to remind me of you!'

Balahvar answered: 'In that case I will take a fresh garment in exchange for my old one. But the difference in value between the old and the new must not be treated as a reward for my pious endeavours, so let the one that you give me be part-worn, like my own.'

Then Iodasaph took a worn vestment and put it on Balahvar, and received his own in exchange. And he said to him: 'You must know that your departure causes me great distress and sorrow.'

39. Balahvar said: 'O prince, I am the servant of Christ our King and not a free agent; His blessings towards me are great, and great is the faith I place in Him. Likewise, my fear of Him cannot be dispelled. I received from Him orders concerning this business, which I must hasten to carry out; if after fulfilling these instructions I postpone the hour of my departure, however reluctant I am to go, I shall be unfaithful to Him. My mission to you is accomplished, now that you have adopted the true creed which I have taught you. All that I have imparted to you is directed towards loyalty to Christ; but now I must withdraw from this assignment of mine to you, and hand over to you responsibility for your own future course of life, for I have expounded to you all His laws. But now I must hasten to other

men, and seek out a fertile field in which to sow the good seed.

'Being on the point of departure, I leave you these rules: Observe the creed which Christ our God has conveyed to you, and prepare yourself for action, that you may fathom His purposes and fulfil His laws. Do not count obedience to Him as any great merit. Do not flatter yourself, nor trust others except those who merit confidence. Distrust and analyze your own impulses, and cast out your lustful desires. Spend the days of your life in such a way that you may be found each day in perfect obedience to God and Our Saviour Jesus Christ, and be prepared to encounter death at any moment. Avoid any deed which may end by involving you in evil and set the seal of sorrow upon your doings. Profit by your youth and bodily vigour to devote yourself to toil and effort, so that lack of time or the onset of sickness may not rob you of the reward of your works by rendering you unfit for any kind of labour. Fulfil God's commands diligently and find humility therein; lay down your head in the place of the despised and sacrifice yourself for the weak. Shun addiction to evil lusts. Do not miss any chance of doing some small good deed by waiting for some greater enterprise to present itself. First thing in the morning, scrutinize critically your own moral qualities and repent of the faults which you have committed the day before. Do not desist from a good deed because the beneficiary is unworthy, but do not emulate wrongful conduct simply because the majority practise it. A wise man should imitate others solely in deeds of goodness. Shun self-satisfaction, and do not congratulate yourself on your own successes. There are, you know, two different ways of being pleased with your good works, one of which brings all manner of virtue in its train, while the other casts a man into all manner of evil. The kind which produces good occurs when a man rejoices at the increasing fruits of his good deeds and his great weariness is relieved by the zeal which he has already shown, which now spurs him on to further feats. What induces all manner of evil is the kind of self-satisfaction which ensues when a man's own works please him greatly, so that his mind is puffed up and gives way to complacency, so that he says: "What I have already done is quite sufficient", and he abandons all future effort. So have more concern for yourself, that you may devise how to escape the fearsome snares of the world, to win liberation and enter on that narrow road which leads to eternal rest!'

40. 'Such are my teachings which I leave you, in loyal fulfilment of my duty towards you and towards God for your sake. I beseech God that He may bestow upon you the fullness of His grace and the excellent virtue of His obedient servants. May He set upon your life and deeds the imprint of all goodness, and grant you self-control so that you do not fall into evil. May He deliver your will from all temptation and protect you beneath the shield of His cross, an impregnable and secure refuge, whereby you will be guarded from phantoms both human and diabolical. May He implant in your heart loathing for this world, and grant you a life of piety in the world below and heavenly bliss in the life to come. May your days be filled with peace and tranquillity and may you be free from all cares for your own sake, until you reach in company with us the supreme abode of the just and the loftiest station of the elect believers. Amen.'

Iodasaph said in reply: 'You call me a king's son. Yet I am no king's son, but a slave and son of a slave of unrighteousness. But God has magnified his benevolence towards me by your agency and has also given me the occasion to enhance your own merits, since you have brought me knowledge of the Lord Jesus Christ, who was conceived without immission of seed and born of the Virgin Mary. You have taught me His holy creed, set me upon the path of truth, stripped off the veil of blindness, and rescued me from the snares of death. Great is the reward I owe you for your kindnesses towards me, and I cannot sufficiently render thanks to you as I ought; but God will recompense you on my behalf, for to Him belongs the fullness of reward. God will bestow His bounty upon you until you are fully satisfied! If you will abide with me, you shall be the delight of my soul. If you depart, may God not cut off your paths from the sphere of His purposes. But let Christ our God make up any deficiency in my gratitude towards you in that place where each man shall utter aloud his paean of praise, and may God the Father of Our Lord Jesus Christ accompany you in all your ways.'

Then they arose to bid one another farewell and took leave of one another and embraced each other with tears. And Balahvar went his way, filled with spiritual joy because his desire was fulfilled. And he gave thanks to Our Lord Jesus Christ, to whom belong glory and honour, thanks and obeisance together with the Father and the most holy life-giving Spirit, now and always and for ever and ever, Amen.[1]

[1] Copyist's note in the manuscript: 'O Christ, have mercy on the soul of David and his parents and brethren, Amen. O Christ, glorify the soul of Prochorus, Theodore and Michael and my spiritual brethren, Michael and Saba, Amen.'

BOOK 3

THE LIFE AND MINISTRY OF THE BLESSED IODASAPH THE KING'S SON, WHOM THE HOLY FATHER BALAHVAR CONVERTED, AND WHO CONVERTED HIS FATHER KING ABENES AND THE LAND OF INDIA TO THE SERVICE OF CHRIST.[1]

41. From thenceforward Iodasaph began to fast and pray and serve God in secret. At the hour when men fall asleep, he would begin to hold vigil until the dawn, and with tears and groans he would perform his seven acts of prayer the whole night through.

But Zadan his servant, whom the king had appointed to look after his son, went away to his own quarters greatly troubled about Iodasaph's affairs, and pretended to be ill. They informed the king about his health, and he was sorry to hear of Zadan's sickness. He appointed one of his trusty retainers to act in Zadan's place, and sent his own physician to Zadan to cure his ailment. But when the physician had examined him, he returned to the king and reported: 'I have been unable to diagnose any ailment in that man. I have examined him all over, and found no symptoms of illness. My opinion is that he must have suffered some grief serious enough to produce such exhaustion in his system, for his forces are at a low ebb.'

When the king heard these words, his face fell and he sensed the reason for Zadan's ailment. He imagined that his son was tired of Zadan's company and had treated him with disfavour and hostility, with the result that Zadan had resigned from his service. So the king sent word to Zadan, saying: 'I have learnt of your illness and am sorry to hear about it, so I propose to come and see you today. So be prepared for my visit!'

When Zadan received this message, he arose at once and put

---

[1] Here the scribe has added another note: 'O Christ, have mercy on David, Amen.'

on his clothes, and went forth to the king. While on his way, he encountered the king, who said to him: 'Why did you not remain at home until my arrival, so that I might perform an act of courtesy towards you?'

Zadan answered and said to the king: 'My distemper, O king, arises not from any ailment, but from pain in my heart. That is why I was unwilling to put Your Majesty to any trouble, since this is not a case of genuine sickness and I have no wish to abuse Your Majesty's kindness.'

The king said: 'Now what is this pain of yours?'

Zadan said: 'A great woe has seized upon me, and a fit of trembling due to a terrible and grievous event.'

The king said: 'Come into the palace, that I may learn the details of this affair from you at leisure.'

When the king had entered into the palace with Zadan, he told Abenes what he had seen and heard of Balahvar the ascetic—how he had been continually instructing the king's son and denouncing the ways of the world, how the prince had cherished his words until he had learnt them by heart and attained to perfection of knowledge, and how Balahvar had catechized him and instructed him in wisdom, until he was fully initiated.

42. At this the king was filled with great anger and dismay. Afterwards he resolved to bide his time patiently, because he planned to resort to a ruse in order to make his son submit once more to his own will. Then he summoned a certain man who was his counsellor, and whose name was Rakhis. (Whenever the king was worried by some troublesome and grievous problem, this man served as the king's comforter.) So now King Abenes told Rakhis his son's story, and asked him insistently for advice regarding him.

Rakhis said to the king: 'Our first step is to make every possible effort to capture Balahvar. If Your Majesty succeeds in apprehending him, we will arrange a debate with Balahvar and show the prince how he is deluded. We will prove that it is wrong to reject those good things which our gods have given us to enjoy and show how this trickster cuts men off from pleasures without which this world is valueless. When we have proved all this and won our case, the prince will be cured of his delusion and this will constitute a victory for us.

'If we fail to track down Balahvar, Your Majesty, I will produce in his stead a certain man who is quite unknown in this land. He is of our creed and indistinguishable from Balahvar in physiognomy, complexion, stature, voice and speech. He dwells outside in the wilderness and his name is Nakhor; and he was my own teacher.'

The king said: 'How is this to be managed?'

Rakhis said: 'I shall sally forth secretly at night, acquaint him with this entire business of ours, and teach him our plan of action. Then he will come out on to the road disguised in monastic dress and appearance. When we engage him in conversation, he shall answer in the language of the monks, and declare his opposition to our creed. When we ask him his name, he shall say: "I am Balahvar!" When we arrange a disputation in the prince's presence, he will imagine that this is really Balahvar, because there will be nothing to distinguish him from that impostor. Then Nakhor will begin by championing that creed of theirs, and reviling ours. But when we reach the conclusion, he will start faltering in his words, admit his error and concede victory for our side over himself. And so Nakhor shall himself prevail on the prince to abandon his course of behaviour and convince him that it is good to build up his city and countries and enjoy the delights thereof, and that quitting the world, voluntarily embracing death, and dooming a man to childless extinction, is a complete fallacy. After all, if all men chose to abandon the world entirely and embrace the monastic life, then in a short space of time the world would be entirely laid waste!—By this scheme, I have every hope of dispelling Your Majesty's worries.'

When the king heard these words of Rakhis, he was greatly cheered, for he hoped to fulfil his desire through Rakhis' counsel. Thereupon the king set out in quest of Balahvar.

43. Sending out his retainers over several different routes, Abenes set out in person on the particular road which Balahvar was most likely to follow. He travelled for many days and found no one, and became very weary and exasperated, and wanted to turn back. Then Rakhis resorted to divination to find out whether they were going to succeed in their search, and told the king: 'Behold, the omens tell us that we shall not turn back

without achieving success! Already I see our quarry approaching us, and success is at hand. If Your Majesty will consent, pray remain here today and send me on in front.' And the king followed his advice and sent him out with a small force of troops.

It was evening. Rakhis caught sight of a group of hermits walking along. When they drew near, they turned out to be a party of the servants of God dwelling in the desert, who had completely abandoned this transitory life for the sake of Christ. The leader of the group carried some dead men's bones hanging from him by an old cord. But Balahvar, whom Rakhis knew by sight, was not among them.

Rakhis said to them: 'Where is that man who has perverted and ruined the king's son?'

The bearer of the relics said to him: 'He is not among us, nor could we tolerate his presence! But he is a much closer neighbour to yourselves!'—And the holy man added: 'In fact, I know that person in question, whose name is Rakhis, and a very devil is he. I imagine that he is of your company!'

Rakhis replied: 'I was asking about Balahvar.'

The holy man retorted: 'Why then did you allege that he has perverted and ruined anyone? Rather should you have said in enquiring about him: "Where is he who has instructed and afforded salvation to such and such a person?" He is our brother and companion, though it is a long time since we last saw him.'

Rakhis said: 'Tell us at least where he is to be found!'

The saint answered him: 'If he had desired to meet you, he would himself have come out to look for you. But we shall not impose any encounter on him against his own wishes.'

Rakhis said: 'The king will put you to death.'

The lover of Christ answered him: 'What pleasure can you see in our way of life which might make us cling to existence in this world, and shrink from death for Christ's sake, with which you seek to terrify us?'

Then Rakhis drove the holy men along and brought them to the king. When the king set eyes on them, he was much perturbed, for he imagined that he had extirpated them from his realm altogether. So the king said to those saints: 'If you are carrying these relics about through love and compassion for those to whom they belong, this very day your own heads and bones can be joined to their number.'

That holy man upon whom the relics hung rejoined: 'We pity and lament our own selves more than those departed ones to whom these relics belong; for they lie at rest, while we languish in bondage in this transitory world. It is because we yearn to join them that we carry their relics about, for they remind us day by day of death.'

The king answered: 'Why should those dried up relics remind wise men of death more effectively than do those bones which you carry about within your own bodies?'

The holy man replied: 'They give more potent warning because they are the relics of dead men, whereas our own bones are living things. If the bones of dead and living men be alike, as you allege, then why do you yourself take no heed of death, seeing that you have bones inside your own body? What crime have you to lay at our door? Again, tell me why you are harrying the saints who have cast aside this transitory world and no longer compete with you for a share in it, and do not rather persecute those who vie with you in partaking of the world's delights?'

The king answered: 'It is because those people are perverted, as well as perverting many others as well, preventing them from enjoying the good things and delights which were created for mankind's sake. This wrath of mine serves as a lesson both for them and for the nation, so that the land may not become waste, and also to punish these ascetics for having no love for the good things of the earth.'[1]

The holy man answered: 'If indeed you censure us because

---

[1] This dialogue between Abenes and the ascetic vividly illustrates the root causes of state hostility to religious sects of Dualist character, such as the Manichaeans. Sir Steven Runciman writes: 'Manichaeanism failed because it was too anti-social. The authorities in that hard bellicose age, with civilization on the defensive against the barbarian invader, could not approve of a faith wherein all killing, even of animals, was forbidden, and whereof a considerable number of believers wandered about, refusing to work, refusing to notice secular regulations, living on the charity of others and exercising a vast influence on the whole community.' And again: 'Thus all good Christians must necessarily fight against Dualism. And the State will usually support them. For the doctrine of Dualism leads inevitably to the doctrine that race-suicide is desirable; and that is a doctrine that no lay authority can regard with approval.' (Steven Runciman, *The Medieval Manichee. A Study of the Christian Dualist Heresy*, Cambridge, 1947, pp. 17, 175.) It seems increasingly apparent that the legend of Barlaam and Josaphat did indeed originate as a Manichaean religious tract.

we have turned our backs on the pleasure of the world, and you desire all men to live in ease, why then do you not give everybody a share in the luxuries which you enjoy? Why do you allow the people to enjoy only those pleasures for which you have no personal use?'

The king replied: 'Because there is no equality between king and slave, duke and commoner. Every man should receive luxury and honour according to his proper status.'

The saint answered: 'By this statement of yours, you flatly contradict yourself! It is evident that you are seeking your own advantage, and not that of people generally. Now if you so desire, I will teach you why you are aflame with the fire of envy and burning to persecute those who have ceased to wear laymen's clothing. You allege that your land will be depopulated through the multiplying of monks. But your real ambition is to bend mankind beneath the yoke of slavery, so that you may reign over them. You want them degraded for the sake of your exaltation, and them to be poor so that your own prosperity may grow according to your desire. You grant them freedom whenever you so please from motives of prestige, or restrict their movements according to your whim, and you set up your caprice as a barrier between yourself and your subjects. You exploit those who hunt after the pursuits of this world in the same way that a man will rear hawks or hounds, and tie them up and starve them so that they may fall with greater ferocity upon their prey. And when they succeed in catching the quarry, the hunter drags it from their mouth and ties them down with cord and chain. Then their success is turned into remorse and their joy to repining, and instead of their being fondled and praised, they are humiliated and driven outside. — In like fashion, you train men to love this world as much as it suits you, and then stop them at your whim from actually enjoying it. The only things you allow your subjects to enjoy are those which you can readily spare. It is clear that you seek your own advantage and not your neighbour's, and this is why you want us to revert to the world.'

The king rejoined: 'Tell me now, have you any superior among your companions?'

The holy man replied: 'There is no one among them superior to me, nor any one inferior, for we are all one through Christ.

This kind of differentiation exists only among you and your associates. Among us, no one is superior to his neighbour in prestige and wealth and nobility, nor is anyone inferior to his neighbour by reason of poverty and privation and low esteem.'

At this point the king ordered their hands and feet to be lopped off and their eyes dug out, and had them cast on to the road in a state between life and death. And he told Rakhis to produce Nakhor, the man who resembled Balahvar.

44. So Rakhis went out alone by night and found Nakhor, and apprised him of the scheme which he and the king had devised. Then he set him upon a horse, but when they were approaching the royal palace, Rakhis left Nakhor and went off to see the king. He told him all about the measures and arrangements which had been agreed on, and how Nakhor was to make his appearance on the road as the king went by.

When it grew light, the king sallied forth from the town for a ride, as was his custom. Nobody knew of the plot except for the king and Rakhis himself. During their ride, they saw a man walking towards them, a bowshot's distance away. This was Nakhor, disguised according to Rakhis's instructions. The king exclaimed: 'Who is that man coming along this way?'

When they brought him to the king, he turned out to be a man resembling those who dwell in the wilderness and follow the monastic order. The king said to him: 'What devil's minion[1] are you?'

The man replied: 'I am no minion of the devil. But if you ask me what manner of person I am, then I will tell you.'

The king said: 'I believe you are Balahvar!'

The false Balahvar retorted: 'If indeed I am he, then I have rendered you no small service.'

The king asked: 'What service do you claim to have rendered me?'

The false Balahvar said: 'My claim is that you wanted your son taught how to attain perdition, whereas I have striven to teach your son the truth, until he has come to know Christ, the God and Saviour of all men, and his own Creator. And he has

---

[1] The Georgian *pahraki*, which I render as 'minion', is in reality an ancient Parthian word, *pahrag*, a sentry or watch-post. (I am indebted to Dr Mary Boyce for elucidating this term for me.)

come to believe in what the prophets, apostles and holy fathers have told us, and what God has prepared for those that love Him as well as for His enemies. Your son himself was formerly an enemy of God, but I have reconciled him with God the Father of Our Lord Jesus Christ. And he has accepted my teaching and preferred it to all your ungodliness.'

Then the king expressed to the assembled company his delight at finding Balahvar. And he said to the false Balahvar: 'I do not propose to kill you until I have held a debate with you. If you recant, then I will pardon your previous error; but if you persist in this same folly of yours, I will expose your delusion before men's eyes, and cause you to die a death of hideous shame and agony.' Then the king told his men to place the hermit on a horse, and they all set off. And the king entered his palace.

It was blazoned abroad that the king had captured Balahvar, and the news of it reached the king's son. The prince was exceedingly sad at heart and greatly afflicted. But a certain grandee, who was secretly a servant of Our Lord Jesus Christ, knew the truth of the matter; his name was Barakhia, and he was a kinsman of the prince. This man saw through their machinations, for he had himself once had an argument with Nakhor on controversial matters of religious belief. So Barakhia visited the prince by night and said to him: 'This man who has been caught is not Balahvar, but his double, indistinguishable from him in appearance and complexion, in voice and speech. His name is Nakhor, and he is a pagan and belongs to the same creed as the king.' And Barakhia went on to outline the king's entire plan, and explained how a trap had been laid for the prince by this method.

Then Iodasaph rejoiced with exceeding gladness and was relieved of the pain which he felt on the holy Balahvar's account. His strength revived sufficiently for him to surmount the pitfalls they had laid for him, and he told Barakhia to reveal the matter to no one.

45. Next morning the king arose and went out to see his son, and said to him: 'My child, no one ever experienced such joy as I felt on your account. No one's joy was ever turned into such bitterness and sorrow as you have brought upon me, for you have cut off the hope which I placed in you, sapped the

strength of my sinews and dimmed the light of my eyes, and you have brought about that very thing I dreaded for your sake. Once I held life of no account, and looked on death with bold eyes, for I counted on your succeeding me after my death. But from now on I shall cling lovingly to life and shun death, for you have falsified my hope and betrayed my trust. You have plunged me into consternation by listening to false preachings, for you have fallen into that very snare which I feared, and from which I used every effort to guard you and keep you away. Instead of inheriting the kingdom, you have chosen in your ignorance, childishness and folly to bring upon yourself your own downfall. Am I not your father and parent? But you have abandoned my faith, opposed my wishes through your wilfulness, cast doubt on the religion of your ancestors, and delivered your downy curls into the hands of false men and seducers, who will lead you into sorrow and hurl you into perdition. Are you not ashamed at having turned to bitterness the joy which I felt on your account? You have not shrunk from breaking my heart! You have scorned to give thanks to the gods for the many boons which they have vouchsafed us, and have not cultivated their favour. You have mortified your father by rejecting his precepts during his lifetime and refusing to succeed him after his death. Yet I suppose there is nothing surprising in this, seeing the times we live in and the prowess of the devil. Neither would it be out of the question even now for you to resume your obedience to your father's will.'

Iodasaph answered and said: 'You have brought to light this business of mine, O king, although I wanted to keep it from you, so that you could go on deriving pleasure from the plans which you made with such loving care. My desire is to conform outwardly in all respects to the pattern which you fondly cherished for me, so that when I die, your heart may not overflow with bitterness because of me. But if you depart this life before me, heaven forbid that you should die robbed of the expectation that I shall succeed you, lest I should send your soul to the grave in sorrow because of me. The sole thing which has deterred me from inviting you to enter God's service and making known to you the faith of Christ is your excessive addiction to sinful ways and your fixed principles of conduct, because of which I felt unable to convert you to the true faith which you find so very obnoxious. Therefore I decided to show my filial respect by concealing from you the fact that I have embraced the faith of Christ with unshakable belief. I wanted to avoid causing you grief and woe, at least until such time as I was forced to reveal the truth, which need then no longer be hidden but would rather help me to overcome all fear and shame before you and prepare me to withstand you. I considered that I was doing my utmost to fulfil your wishes in outward behaviour, conforming as I have done to your ordinances in regard to the steeds I rode, the clothes I wore and the food I ate, and this should be sufficient for you, without your making any demands on my inner self. Your Majesty must realize that though discovery of this secret of mine causes you grief at present, in future it will bring you abounding pleasure and joy for ever. Now leave me in peace to pursue this matter upon which I have embarked, rather than visiting me with wrath and shame. Accept this offer of mine to obey your will in outward forms, without advertising our differences in public. Do not expect me to adopt your religion, and abstain from enquiry into my private convictions, which can do you no harm during your lifetime or after your death.'

When the king heard his son's words, he uttered curses and began to revile and threaten him, saying: 'You proud and wilful young fellow! I shielded you from contact with common humanity and kept you apart from all suffering, so that you might enjoy honour and ease. I protected you from the snares and instigations of the devil. I have pampered your body with tenderness and your eyes and ears with delight, and have spared you all occasion for worry—all this for your personal benefit. But you are puffed up with audacity, and find pleasure and ease irksome. In your ignorance, you chase after suffering and privation! The life you are seeking is such that if you actually taste the flavour of it and experience its sufferings and privations and the many vexations which it holds out for the soul, then you will come to your senses, and your impatience to escape from it will be greater than your present anxiety to flee from the pleasures and comforts of life. Those astrologers were right to prophesy at your birth that you would prove a knave and a wretch, a tiresome and fickle person, and one who refuses to appreciate the good things of the earth. But I gave you a first-class upbringing, that you might grow accustomed to the best things of life. I drove away from you all those deceivers and impostors, and utterly cleansed my land from them, and silenced men's tongues from making any mention of their fraud. When I had revealed to my subjects the evil and false nature of those anchorites, they banished them with ignominy and rooted them out once for all.

'Then the devil armed himself against us. His only chance of prevailing over us lay in vanquishing you, because he found nobody among us more easily vulnerable than yourself, and that is why he put these evil ideas into your head. Can it be that through my guarding and cherishing of you, I have myself exposed you to that very danger which I so much feared for your sake? If only I had exposed you to temptation and forced you to eat the sour together with the sweet, you would not have remained ignorant of the bitterness of affliction and of the sweet savour of pleasures. But now you are oblivious of the sweetness of this life, because you have never yet experienced the bitterness of that existence after which you quest.'

Iodasaph answered and said: 'I cannot tell why Your Majesty is so indignant. Is it on account of the good thing which I have received, or because of my opposition to your will? If you are angry at my finding the good, then I shall have to flee away from you and free myself from your authority. If you are blaming me for opposing your will, and prefer me to be destroyed in conformity with your will rather than to live a life which does not conform to your outlook—then this attitude shows up your indifference towards me, and I myself, if this be truly so, must abandon all trust in you. The grief which Your Majesty feels for me over the good things which I have won is no greater than the grief which I feel on your account, because you are cut off from those eternal blessings. I have more right to sorrow and grief over your lot than you over mine! You have said that I am a mere child. Would that this childish nature of mine might serve as my excuse at the day of judgment! As for the curses which you have poured out upon me, I am content to be reviled, so long as I am spared from all other forms of vileness. If you carry into action your threat towards me, I place my trust in God that I shall be united with that band of holy martyrs to whom your persecutions have brought life eternal.

'What profits it me for you to treat me like a child when I have already reached the age when I can no longer plead my childishness as an excuse? Why should I repine at the curses and foul language which you use towards me? The things for which you rail and storm at me are in fact my joy and pride. What is the use of threatening me with torments? After all, I have voluntarily chosen to endure no little torment on this earth by means of self-mortification, and that is why you are so enraged against me. As for what you say about the boons you have bestowed upon me, Your Majesty should realize that it is those transitory favours of yours which have aroused my desire for the eternal boons of the immortal King. If you force me to abandon those other eternal and unspeakable delights for the sake of these perishable blessings which you give, you must know that there is no comparison between things perishable and things imperishable. As for these gifts of yours, you yourself might well take them away from me because of some trifling annoyance. In any case, the passage of time will sweep away both you and me. But concerning the joy everlasting, Our Lord Jesus Christ speaks thus: "And no one shall take your joy from you."[1]

'The career and life which you chose for me would be fair and beautiful indeed, but for the fact that it passes speedily away. If you can be certain that it is permanent, it is exceedingly good and desirable. But since you cannot guarantee this, why should you not forgive me if I choose to renounce it, thereby to attain the life which is most to be desired? Why are you astonished, O king, at my yearning for eternal blessings, rather than being amazed at your own attachment to the transitory pleasures of this world?

'You state that you have driven away from me the impostors, deceivers and charlatans and silenced men's tongues from making any mention of them. This would certainly have been a very great favour to have done me, if only you had applied these epithets to those who deserve them. But the truth is that you drove away from me the holy priests of Christ and the

---

[1] John, xvi. 22.

blessed Fathers and mentors of my life, and set me down in a desert and waterless place without any spiritual teacher and intercessor, among the serpents and the scorpions, the wild beasts and the devils. Fearing for my sake, you rose in opposition to Christ the true God, and exterminated those righteous Saints of His and elect teachers of salvation who spurned this world. You left me alone to the mercies of the real impostors, deceivers and liars! But God the omnipotent, Father of my Lord and Saviour Jesus Christ, gave me knowledge through His Holy Spirit to attain to understanding of His most holy essence.

'You went on to speak of my desperate, wretched and fickle character, and my boredom with the world and failure to appreciate its benefits. But why should I not be desperate, seeing that despair of this world induces peace, comfort and rest? And this wretchedness of mine here below is in fact an advantage, in that it ensures me life eternal and unending. How could I fail to tire of this world, seeing that the world itself wearies of those people who are in love with it? How could I avoid being fickle towards the world, seeing that the world itself is fickle in its treatment of mortal men, and even you yourself are bound to feel the manifold effects of its fickleness? Or why should I rely on its benefits, seeing that these benefits are bad? Today it bestows them and tomorrow takes them away, and then extracts retribution for them.

'So now, O king, you should take good thought for yourself. Great is God's mercy towards you and the patience with which He waits for your repentance. But you defy Him, oppose His faith and reject His blessings, while He desires mankind to turn unto true repentance. For this reason, He has refrained from punishing your arrogance, nor has He abandoned you to the fecklessness and evil to which you have surrendered yourself nor exacted retribution for your treatment of the Saints, His servants.'[1]

Then the king realized that his own wrath was merely inflaming that of his son, and feared that Iodasaph's outburst would rob him of his self-control. So he arose abruptly and

---

[1] Marginal note by the scribe: 'This is the way to denounce the godless, and those that love this world!'

went off to his palace weighed down with sorrow, beset with woe and overwhelmed with consternation.

46. On the next day, the king came again to his son, clasped him to his bosom and embraced his neck and said: 'O my son, flesh of my flesh, it is unworthy of you to cast doubt on my integrity in all our discussions and accuse me of willingly abandoning the better course, choosing the path of perdition and preferring falsehood to truth. You know full well the firmness and resolute character of my mind. If you were to allege that the laws of truth were irksome to me, and that therefore I was lured into caprice and self-indulgence, the fact is that you and everyone else must admit how patiently I observe the dictates of my own religion. Many a time I have emptied my treasure houses to build temples for the idols and their ministers, and donated all my riches to them, and many a time I have treated with veneration a man of humble birth when I have known him to walk virtuously the path of my religion. I would even arise from my throne and step forward to greet him, and remain standing before him like a slave—just as a slave might stand in front of his lord. Now if my only aim was to enjoy myself, as you profess to believe, why ever should I have exterminated men vowed to repentance, who have quitted worldly enjoyment and left it entirely in my hands, and who asked for no share of it nor vied with me for anything whatsoever? For killing and torture occur only when men are wrathful and exasperated: in a state of exasperation, turmoil agitates the heart and passion the soul, and the mind is painfully excited.

'What foolish wretch could possibly fall into a delusion such as that which you attribute to your own father—namely to be so addicted to passions and lusts as to promulgate them as a body of religious dogma and then lavish his treasures on those who profess it, and sharpen his sword against those who oppose it? What is more, you know the rectitude of my judgment and the justice which I mete out to widows, comfort to orphans, alms to the poor and crippled, and how I myself bear their infirmities for them, and distribute my wealth amongst them. You are aware that on my frequent encounters with the poor and maimed, or with widows and orphans, I can never pass by them without making full provision for their need. How then, my child, could you come to hate my faith and conceive such distrust towards me? How can you assert that I have erred from the path of righteousness, chosen an unworthy course of conduct, and taken up my stand upon the road of iniquity? How is it that you question my tested percipience and known discernment, my sound judgment in recondite matters and my ability to solve dubious questions, while trusting blindly in your own perception? Yet it is clear that some precipitate impulse has suddenly altered your whole outlook, without your examining the matter, nor even referring it to some wise counsellor or learned teacher, or some loyal confidant or judicious man of experience! How can you be so certain that the devil has not seen through your stupidity and weakness and exalted you as if you had attained to divine knowledge, while in reality, he has been laying a snare for you through the tongue of his accomplice, Balahvar? How else can you account for this affair, into which Satan has lured you in your ignorance? How is it that without recourse to a just arbiter, to reliable witnesses or to any intelligible evidence, you venture to conclude that truth is on your side and falsehood on mine? In this, my son, you resemble one of those pious devotees whose ears have been assailed by falsehood, and they have gone astray because of the very novelty of it. Later on, they have had insight into the truth, but falsehood having once caught on has by now taken root within their heart, so that they persist in regarding errors as more true than truth itself. So now you too must beware, my son! I know that your heart inclines towards virtue, and this is the greatest blessing which the gods can vouchsafe to you and through you to us also, for the noble tradition of your fathers will have prevailed upon you!'—And the king went on to enumerate all his ancestors by name, and taught Iodasaph their pedigree and related their life stories to him.[1]

When Iodasaph heard the king's words, he understood that

---

[1] In the Arabic *Book of Bilauhar and Budasaf*, from which our Georgian text is thought to derive, there follows here a long account by King Janaisar (Abenes) of the doings of his royal ancestors Baisam, Shabakhna, Talzin and Filantin, who are portrayed as faithful followers of al-Budd (the Buddha). See *Povest' o Varlaame i Iosafe*, trans. Rosen, Moscow, 1947, pp. 133-8. This fact strengthens one's conviction that the author of the Georgian Christian version had an ancient Arabic text before his eyes.

the devil was laying a snare for him and that he must prepare to muster all his strength to combat the evil one. So he said to the king: 'There is nothing which I desire more, O king, than to reconcile my own welfare with your convictions. But if in spite of all my striving, I fail to conform to your beliefs, I must nevertheless have regard to my own salvation, however much this may displease you. I used to imagine that Your Majesty's command of language was lucid, vigorous and devoid of error, even though in practice, your deeds are false. But now it is obvious that the infirmity of your mind and outlook is even more grievous and severe than the sickness which affects your practical behaviour. My present duty, O king, is to make every effort to counteract your present trend of thought through the agency of wisdom, which is a quality by no means alien to it, for I am bound to feel concern for your mind's sake and must seek out a cure for it. I have no desire to transgress the bounds of courtesy by the candour with which I address Your Majesty. At the same time, anyone who speaks to you with base flattery is no loyal subject of yours.

'Now calm away your indignation and examine your own best interests! You must realize that you are fated soon to die and leave all your worldly glory to others, just like all other mortals who have already departed this life and left their belongings to others. Afterwards you will be raised up once more, and called upon to give an account of your words and deeds. Now there are none remaining in this world who have spoken and taught the right doctrine and put it into practice except for those men who are servants of Christ the Lord and abide in the wilderness, and who believe in the Holy Trinity and its sacred creed. Those hermits have knowledge of the retribution which is due to each individual person, be it bliss or be it torment. Now choose some learned exponent of your religion, and let us hold a formal disputation together concerning the true faith, until truth has been distinguished from falsehood.'

When the king had listened to these words of his son, he was dumbfounded. As soon as he recovered his wits, he started to ponder and reflect, and to struggle against his own impulses. But he was sore beset by his desires, which fought him hard and reminded him of the pleasures and ease to which he was accustomed; and his inward voice spoke to him, saying: 'You cannot exist a single day without the things you are used to, and if you admit your error and change your convictions, you will incur bitterness and reproach.' So he abandoned all hope of departing from his existing habits, and could think of no other course than to serve and glorify the idols.

Then the king said to his son: 'My child, what you have said has intrigued me and converted me to your point of view. Now I must enquire into your words without delay, and investigate them calmly. If they turn out to be true, then they will shine forth the more brightly in the course of my examination. But if they be false, their error will be shown up. So I propose to gather the people together and hold a debate in a spirit of equity, not of violence. I will command the herald to proclaim an amnesty to all the Christians, who belong to your faith, so that they may come to my assembly for a just verdict to be reached there in the presence of the whole nation. Nobody must have grounds for imagining that I have used coercion or for declaring: "Had I attended that assembly myself, I should have uttered a triumphant oration by which the entire people would have been quite convinced and our cause completely vindicated!"'

47. Iodasaph was reassured by the king's speech, and they made arrangements for the assembly. On that day, there was a great concourse. The ministers of the idols came out to lend their support to Nakhor, who was feigning to be Balahvar, as we have mentioned earlier, and whom Rakhis had enlisted on his side. But no one from among the professing Christians attended the gathering, except for a certain man who followed the faith of Our Lord Jesus Christ in secret. His name was Barakhia—that same man of whom we have spoken earlier, who told Iodasaph about the conspiracy framed by Nakhor at the time when the latter was brought in from the wilderness disguised as Balahvar. And Barakhia was ready to support Balahvar in case he wavered at any stage in the debate.

The king took his seat upon his throne, but Iodasaph sat upon the ground, for he had no wish to be seated on a throne. First the king began to address the idol-worshippers and said: 'Behold, you are the heads of this faith, which we have received from you, and wherein we have followed your precepts. Strive to vindicate this faith today! And if your victory be made manifest and decisive, good will be the reward which I shall bestow upon you, as a worthy recognition of your righteousness. But if your discourse is shown to be a pack of falsehood and lies, no one will be deemed so impudent as you and no one will have incurred such guilt as yourselves, both in regard to me personally and in regard to the entire nation, O ministers of the idols. I have made a vow to the gods that if today your doctrine is shown to be false, and you are justly declared to have been vanquished by your opponents, then I shall break my crown, overturn my throne, shave off the hair from my head and join the ranks of the monks. I shall burn those gods of yours with fire and exterminate you, their acolytes; and your houses shall be pillaged and your children given into bondage. And I shall hang your bodies from the gibbet. But if you can avoid being defeated, then your punishment too can be averted.'

Iodasaph said in response: 'O king, you have promulgated a just decree, and no one has the right to carry justice into execution but a monarch. However, I deem it my duty also to imitate Your Majesty's example, for you have decided rightly.' Then Iodasaph said to Nakhor, who was feigning to be Balahvar: 'Behold, you know, O Balahvar, amid what luxury and delights you found me, and how you called upon me to adopt your creed, assuring me of your sincere attachment to it. And I abandoned my humility towards the king and overcame my fear of him, and resigned myself to a life spent in austerity; and I followed you for the sake of my desire for the kingdom of heaven which you preached to me, guaranteeing it to be everlasting, and also for fear of the perpetual torments with which you threatened me. Behold now, the multitude of our foes is gathered together and there is no one among this crowd to lend me aid. You have heard the king's equitable declaration, and I too shall act with complete impartiality. If you have been laying some trap for me to deprive me of the worldly enjoyments which are given to men for their comfort, and have cast me by your wiles into damnation; if again you are defeated in this disputation by a true verdict or through the weakness of your cause, then I shall instantly vent my wrath on your heart and tongue, for I shall tear them out with my own hands and cast them to the dogs, which are readier to tolerate deceit and vilification than are royal princes. This oath I utter before God and His angels, and verily you shall not escape from my hands!'

When Nakhor heard these words of Iodasaph's, he realized that he had fallen into the snare which he himself had dug, and perceived the evil fate and perdition which faced him, now that death threatened him from both sides. He saw that his only hope of avoiding doom lay in employing his whole heart and strength to support and advocate the creed of Balahvar, and thereby pacify the king's son. He was confident that the king would pardon him, in view of the plot they had framed together. So Nakhor opened his lips and began to denounce the idols and their acolytes and then to praise the faith of the Christians and their sacred laws. Such a pitch of devastating eloquence did his speech attain, with such cogency of repartee, that even Balahvar himself could not have equalled it, nor could any of the devotees of the idols refute Nakhor on a single point in his oration.[1]

At this the blessed Iodasaph was joyful in spirit. His face became radiant through the grace of the Holy Spirit, and he thanked and glorified God, the Father of Our Lord Jesus Christ, who had fortified His religion through the mouth of His adversaries.

The debate between them continued for a long time. King Abenes was filled with indignation at Nakhor's success, but was ashamed to wreak vengeance upon him in the people's presence for fear that his own unjust behaviour should be exposed to public view. So the king reflected: 'I have brought this evil upon myself!' Thereupon the king began himself to speak and argue with Nakhor. Since he expressed himself with hot-tempered force and in angry tones, Nakhor took fright, thinking that the king resented the extent of his superiority in this debate, and this hampered him in formulating his arguments. This in turn encouraged the idolaters, for Nakhor began to give way of his own accord through fear of the king. And the king and all his subjects followed the debate with bated breath. Evening drew on while the debate was still in progress, and victory

---

[1] At this point, the Greek version inserts into the narrative the text of a very cogent defence of the Christian religion called the *Apology of Aristides*, attributed to a second century Athenian philosopher of that name. Thereby the author of the Greek version enhanced the effect of this episode and gave concrete evidence for Nakhor's prowess against the idol-worshippers.

was not yet made manifest on either side. The prince for his part, fearing that Nakhor would fall victim to the king's cruelty, readily forgave him for flagging in his opposition to King Abenes.

At length Iodasaph said to King Abenes: 'Today, O king, you have started off this business on the basis of justice! So let it be completed on the same footing. Now grant me one of two alternatives: either hand over my teacher to me, so that he may abide with me, and we may labour together on the principles of our faith, and so that he may be free from intimidation, lest the voice of truth be silenced by fear. And do you take your own mentors with you, and do with them whatever you desire. Or else deliver your counsellors to me, and take my master to yourself. But if you take both your advisers and mine away with you, then yours will be in tranquillity, but mine will be cut off from me and remain a prey to terror and tribulation. Such a proceeding would be tyrannical and unjust.'

The king was reluctant to leave his high priests with the prince his son, for fear that the latter might convert them from idolatry by means of his eloquence. Still hoping that Nakhor would secretly find means to carry into effect the stratagem they had plotted together, the king handed Nakhor over to his son. The prince went off into his palace and took Nakhor along with him. And the entire people still imagined that Nakhor was really Balahvar.

Then Prince Iodasaph said to Nakhor secretly in the night: 'I know that you are really Nakhor and not Balahvar, but I have shielded you, Nakhor! Be glad rather, for today you have done much good work and greatly furthered the faith of our sacred Lord by your eloquence. Now I have taken you away to protect you from the king's vengeance. However, if your lips are unwilling, we have no desire to avail ourselves of their help on behalf of our religion. Rely rather on your own intelligence, give ear to the gospel message of God's Son, turn with sincerity to confess Christ and His religion and wait for the rewards and retribution which He metes out, for you must soon pass away just as earlier generations passed away. Beware of choosing perishable joys in preference to those imperishable delights which flow from Christ!'

Nakhor said: 'I am ready, O king's son, to accept what you

urge upon me. I believe in God and recognize that all things owe their existence to Him, and that He metes out eternal retribution to mankind according to their deeds. I prostrate myself before God because of my sins, for He is the Prince of mercy. I know that you are sincere in exhorting me to follow this course. Even previously I have been aware of the truth, but I followed my own inclinations and was reluctant to depart from the faith and the evil customs of my ancestors. Rejoice, O prince, in God's favour and in His good rewards which you will receive if you perform His will. And I advise you to honour your father and live together with him in a conciliatory spirit, until God provides a way for you to follow. The nature and object of our plot is known to you, O prince. What words can I address to the king if I encounter him, in view of the shame which I must needs feel in his presence? I have failed completely to justify the hopes which he placed in me! So now I beg you to let me depart and abide in the wilderness with the servants of Christ. If the Lord wills it, I will come again to see you in a little while.'

The king's son gave his permission and bade him go in peace. After saying goodbye to Iodasaph, Nakhor departed full of faith in Christ, and inspired with deep repentance for his previous misguided conduct. And he dwelt among the hermits according to the true monastic rites and rules. All who heard of this offered up praise to Christ our God.

When the news about Nakhor reached King Abenes, he fell into despair, now that he had lost all hope of converting his son through Nakhor's agency. So the king deferred for a time the debate with his son, and began to despise the cult of idols and expressed contempt for them on numerous occasions, as well as lack of respect for their acolytes. However, he could not quite bring himself to adopt the way of God's service for himself. Iodasaph for his part treated the king with friendly kindness, as Nakhor had advised him, and never rebuked him for his behaviour.

48. A few days later, the grand festival of the idols fell due. The king used formerly to impart great pomp to this event. But now that the pagan priests saw how the king despised the idols and their acolytes, they feared that he might not attend their

celebration nor offer any sacrifice to the idols, to their intense humiliation. Therefore they arose and went to a certain man who dwelt in the wilderness among the mountains and had renounced and rejected the life of the world and the flesh. His name was Thedma, and he was an adherent of their faith. The king and his whole people greatly relied on him, to the point of imagining that rain and sunshine were granted to their country according to his prayers. So they brought the hermit to the king to give him encouragement and banish doubt and despondency from his heart.

The king caught sight of Thedma as he entered his presence, wearing no clothes except for an old rag girding his loins, and leaning on a staff. It was a long time since the king had seen the hermit, so he jumped up quickly as soon as he set eyes on him, fell down before him and adored him, and embraced his legs. Then he stood up before him as a slave stands before his master, until Thedma bade him be seated. The king sat down, and Thedma answered and said to the king: 'Your Majesty! May you live through the power of the idols. I have heard that you have striven doughtily in the campaign against the devils. I was delighted when I learnt that victory was granted to you.'

The king said: 'No victory was accorded us at all! Never did we stand in such need of warriors and knights as we do today. Now what help can we expect from you?'

Thedma answered: 'It is fitting first of all for us to celebrate the great festival which is at hand, rendering to the gods due tribute for all the victories and successes which they bestow. Only after this should we engage the foe and struggle steadfastly against him, being equipped afresh with all the armoury needed to assure us victory.'

FABLE THE FOURTEENTH

The Amorous Wife

The king said to Thedma: 'Your situation and mine resemble that of a certain military commander who possessed a most attractive wife. Now that man was extremely jealous in regard to women and feared that his wife might become frustrated and be unfaithful to him. So he said to the lady: "I know the fickleness and weakness of womankind. I have an enemy after me, who is coming to seduce you. So watch out and be firm. And I will give you a signal.—Whenever you feel an urge for sexual intercourse, let your hair down. When I see this sign, I will give battle to the foe and satisfy your desire, and his rage shall not triumph over you!"

'The woman acted accordingly, and they lived together for a long time without any sin being committed. But one day foemen approached and there was an alarm, and the warriors sallied forth to repulse the enemy. So our hero too arose and donned his armour. When his wife saw him decked out in his panoply, she was filled with sexual desire, for that hero was a splendid knight. So the woman gave the signal which she had learnt from her husband. When the man saw this, he went back into his house and stayed there until he had quenched his wife's passion. After this, he sallied forth to encounter the foe. By the time he emerged, the army was already returning from the fray. The soldiers started to rail at him and say: "You were too frightened to sally out, until you heard that we had put the enemy to flight!" But the champion said to them: "My private foe was battling with me! I could not leave him in order to fight outside enemies, for he was my most domestic and immediate foe. Now that I have conquered him, I can rejoin your company."

'Thus it is with us, O Thedma! Today we are involved in an affair which affects both us and the idols. But first of all I have to exterminate my own personal enemies. If afterwards we establish that the idols are really gods, then we shall offer up sacrifices to them. But if they cannot be proved genuine deities, what can such imaginary beings profit us?'

Thedma retorted: 'There is no more reliable coat of mail or sharper sword to use against enemies than the celebration of festival rites. No measures can bring you nearer to victory than offering up sacrifices to the idols. Thereby you will be fortified against all and every foe.'

The king replied: 'I have been wondering and fearing that it is the true faith itself which we have been fighting. However, if you so wish, then you can go and celebrate the festival. But I shall remain sceptical until it is revealed to me what course is best. Otherwise, you are welcome to reveal the truth to me, if you have some firm evidence in your hands. If you can disperse the misgivings from my heart, then I too will join you in celebrating the holiday festivities.'

At this, Thedma was enraged. He threw down the staff which he held in his hand, tore off the rags which he had wound round his loins, entwined his fingers together, and stood naked in front of the king, and said to him: 'If you have no love for your kingdom, O king, and are turned into a slave; if you have abandoned splendour for poverty and luxury for hardship; if you are resolved not to spare that pampered and cosseted body of yours and propose to quit all this comfort for the sake of embracing misery to which you are not accustomed and will never be able to endure—then I am made of even sterner stuff. I can easily cast away this stick and these rags, but shall not yield to falsehood. I am not afraid of the monastic path, because there is no existence more austere and harsh than my life, which I patiently endure. This world has nothing to demand from me, nor have I anything to demand from this world, apart from the earth on which I crawl along, and the grass on which I nourish myself. So let us set out together, Your Majesty, for your mind has hit upon a good idea!'

When the king heard these words of Thedma, he despaired of getting help from him and realized how impotent was their faith. And the brood of doubt multiplied within his heart. He resolved to confess the true God, and began to ponder and meditate within himself. But as he was considering the matter in his mind, there arose within him the spirit of love of this world, which recalled to him the varied flavours and enjoyments which are forbidden by the Christian faith. And he was overcome by his old habits, to which he had ever been in bondage. So he gave orders for preparations to be made for the festival, according to established custom.

49. When the festival was over, the king asked Thedma: 'How are we going to set about converting my son?'

FABLE THE FIFTEENTH

The Youth who had never seen a Woman

Thedma answered the king: 'You must get devils to operate on him through the wiles of women, for these can wound the spirit more deeply than a two-edged sword.[1] I once heard of a certain king who had a son. And the physicians declared to that monarch: "If the child sees the sun before he is ten years old, the light of his eyes will be extinguished, for we observe that their pupils are weak of vision." So the king hollowed out a cave in the ground and ordered his son to be brought up there in company with his nurse. When the boy was ten years old, he had him brought out. Since the lad had never set eyes on any other living being, his father ordered a specimen of every kind of creature to be set before him one by one, so that he might learn the identity of each one that he saw. In addition, finely arrayed girls were to be placed in his path. And they did so.

'The boy asked about every kind of being, and they gave him information about them. He also enquired about the girls. They told him: "Those are devils which agitate and ruin men!' The boy was filled with longing for those devils. His father asked the lad: "What was the most beautiful thing you saw during your walk?" The boy replied: "I have seen nothing fairer than those devils, and there is nothing I desire more than them!"— So now there is nothing which will avail Your Majesty better than ravishing maidens, whom you should introduce to his presence at all times of day, so that the devil may exercise his powers through their agency.'

Then the king ordered all his son's retainers to be removed from his palace, and replaced them with beautiful and comely girls chosen from every quarter of his domains to act as Iodasaph's servants. Then the prince's palace was filled with their allurements. The king's son suffered greatly from their efforts to beguile him, and his mind was disturbed in a way which he had never known before. The king told these girls to sing and entice him at all times of the day and night, so they decked themselves out and tantalized him with every kind of temptation with which they sought to arouse his appetites. They were very zealous in carrying out the king's instructions. Sometimes they would exhibit themselves in male disguise, sometimes put on armour and parade in front of him, or else they would take on the guise of hunters or of musicians, with harps and trumpets and cymbals, and besiege his ears with all kinds of melodies. At other times they would invade his room

[1] Proverbs, v. 4.

stark naked and lure him on with lascivious talk, urging him to sally forth a-hunting or go for a walk in the gardens of delight. Whenever the prince went out, the girls also mounted their steeds and scampered round about him. In all this, they were fulfilling the king's instructions, and they succeeded in shaking his convictions more than any eloquence of man could have done.

Now among these girls was a certain king's daughter, who had been brought as a captive to King Abenes. She was fairer than all the others and more intelligent than they; and the prince fell in love with her because of her beauty and wisdom, since she was extremely clever and resourceful. The prince would often discuss religious problems with her and talk of the transitory nature of this world, reminding her of God and condemning the error of the idolaters. When the king heard of this, he was delighted to hear of Iodasaph's love for this maiden, for he imagined that he would prevail over his son through her influence.

One day the girl said to Iodasaph: 'If you want me to pay heed to your exhortations, O prince, then grant me but one year's solace in your arms. I promise you that I shall then confess your faith, and both of us will serve your God until our death.'

Iodasaph said to the maid: 'And whence shall come my recompense if death should overtake me before the year is up?'

The girl answered: 'If death should overtake you, you will be rewarded by the fact that I have been converted. You will not be held guilty for following my desire, for you yourself say: "Marriage is honourable in all."'[1]

Iodasaph said: 'That is so, but I should not win the grace of self-denial with those who have endured and quenched the furnace of the flesh. What is more, I fear that self-indulgence might entice me into some worse enterprise, or that sin might rule me and hurl me into damnation, or that I might turn out to be an enemy of God and a friend of the devil.'

The woman replied: 'Spend one month with me, or even one night, and I will fulfil all your command and desire. Surely so

[1] Hebrews, xiii. 4.—Note by the copyist: 'Christ, deliver us from the snares of the devil.'

trifling an indulgence as this cannot affect the reward due to you for recovering an erring soul, reconciling it with God, and procuring for it salvation after death?'

Iodasaph was favourably disposed to carry out her request, because his natural instincts inclined him to do so. He made her swear that she would confess God's faith. His reason was taken captive by their mutual passion, which threw his mind entirely off balance. But Our Lord Jesus Christ came to his rescue and would not let him go to his damnation, according to the words of the Psalmist David: 'I inclined to fall violently, and the Lord caught me with his hand; and had the Lord not come to my help, my soul would straightway have found itself in Hell.'[1]

Plunged in thought, Iodasaph spent the night in vigil, praying to God that He would assist him and open to him the door of righteousness, and then he dropped off to sleep. Blessed is God, who fulfils the desire of those that fear Him! As he slumbered, Iodasaph had a vision. He dreamt that he had arrived in the kingdom of Heaven and saw the many-coloured delights, the gilded temples and all the attendant luxury, far surpassing anything which is to be seen in this world upon earth. And then at the side he caught sight of those women his tempters, whose wiles had wounded his soul. In comparison with the joys of paradise, their faces seemed to him more hideous and unsightly than dogs' or pigs' snouts. The prince heard a voice saying: 'This is the abode of rest for the saints and the steadfast, and here they shall enjoy eternal ease.' Afterwards they took him into hell and he saw the terrible torments suffered by each sinner there, which nobody can enumerate except God who devised them. Again he heard a voice saying: 'This is the retribution of godless mortals and sinners, who had abandoned Christ our God and fallen in love with this world. Here they shall be tormented for ever and for all eternity.'

When Iodasaph awoke and opened his eyes, he saw the girls standing round him weeping and lamenting, for they imagined that he had died in the course of that prolonged dream. Iodasaph arose and began to examine their attractions. And he was amazed how insignificant and ugly they appeared to his eyes compared with those joys which he had beheld in his vision.

The king came to visit his son, because he had heard about

[1] Cf. Psalm xciv. 17.

this incident; and he enquired what Iodasaph had seen, and what thoughts were in his mind. So Iodasaph told him everything which he had witnessed in paradise, its beauties and unparalleled delights. Afterwards he told him what he had seen in hell, and its unbearable and fearsome torments. Then he said to the king: 'My father, I wish to go away into the wilderness and live as a monk among the hermits and there to serve the life-giving God, because of my desire for that felicity and my fear of those torments which I have seen.'

50. When the king heard his son's words, he was cast down with grief and filled with mortification. Unable to bear this or to conceal his feelings, he cried aloud before all the people and said: 'Never has a greater or more terrible evil befallen me and yourselves than this tragedy of my son. If some monarch or potent enemy were to kidnap my son, we should not submit to this, nor would we spare our own lives in his defence. We should sacrifice ourselves unreservedly, as both I and yourselves are bound to do for my son's sake. You recall how I persecuted the enemies of our religion, and how I killed them and burnt them with fire. And now I fear that if the boy is going to run wild and start associating with the anchorites as a result of his ignorance and folly, then one of my enemies may slay him. If I exact vengeance for his blood, I shall then be condemned for injustice! Having once tried to exterminate the hermits, how can I now abandon my own son to their tender mercies? If I give in, then the reproach of weakness will remain upon me and yourselves for ever, and we shall be turned into a laughing stock for our foes. If only we could find a man capable of solving this problem with which I am burdened—one who could teach me how to treat the boy and afford me aid in these troubles of mine —then I would grant him respect and honour greater than what is accorded to myself. We must not neglect this matter nor relax our efforts until we succeed in finding out the truth about our son, and how we ought to deal with him.'

Thereupon the dignitaries and grandees said to Abenes: 'No effort must be spared to solve this problem in all its aspects; for there is none more eager to secure your happiness than we are, nor anyone more affected than we are by Your Majesty's troubles! But in our opinion it is not feasible to divide one single realm between two opposing religions, two creeds, and two legal systems. We shall never achieve success unless we light upon a solution whereby your son, your religion and your kingdom may all jointly be restored to health.' And they continued to enlarge on this theme.

Eventually the king and all his dukes decided to give half his kingdom to the prince for him to reign over. The king acted thus in order to lay a snare for Iodasaph, calculating that through transacting affairs of state, he would become wrapped up in worldly matters and fall a prey to earthly lusts.

However, Iodasaph saw through their wily ruses, but was delighted at the prospect of being enabled to revive the faith which his father had suppressed, openly to preach the gospel of Our Lord Jesus Christ, and to reunite all His faithful people and strive energetically to hold fast to all the precepts of Christianity. Iodasaph found this prospect highly encouraging.

The king said to Iodasaph: 'My son, this was not the kind of future which I mapped out for you! I fancied that you would be the light of my existence and my successor after my death. But you have dashed my hopes, openly resisted me and turned the sweetness of my joy in you into bitterness; and you have severed the paternal heart-strings which united my breast with yours. But I feel myself unable to resist your plea, for the bonds of parenthood incline me in your favour and oblige me to act according to your desires, and to avoid any deeds which are uncongenial to you. You refuse to pardon my faults as I pardon yours, nor will you grieve at parting from me, as I grieve for your sake. May you live and prosper wherever you may be! I am fully aware that by letting you go, I am humiliating and deceiving myself. I am fulfilling your desire because of the love of their offspring which reigns in the depths of their fathers' hearts, so that they submit to their children's behests even though they are in opposition to their own wishes.

'Thus it is also with a man who gives in to his own inclinations, even though he knows that they bring blame and harm upon himself; but he conceals his faults from men while finding excuses for himself, forgetting his own shortcomings and priding himself on what little virtue he manages to retain. But I, my son, although I am a king, am also a man. My heart is tender towards you, as is the way with all men towards their children. I cannot go on opposing you, any more than I can oppose my own will. You have brought down great evil upon my head and your own. But my main wish is to bring this matter to the most successful conclusion possible, to do what you desire, and seek to cure you and myself in peace and tranquillity. So now I appoint you king over half my realm. Administer it yourself as you will. Only let not our enemies mock nor the envious rejoice at your estrangement from me, nor let me be completely without posterity from you, lest your extinction make me suffer death before my time comes to pass away! But if you make your kingdom prosper and manage your affairs skilfully, my soul will not be altogether desolate because of you. And may your doings be attended perpetually with peace, good health, and success.'

51. The youth answered the king and said: 'I have paid heed to your words, O king. May God strengthen you with the spirit of peace and vouchsafe the best of prosperity to your life and reign. However, I cannot accept that authority which you bestow upon me, being unaccustomed to such responsibility and quite devoid of any taste for transitory glory. I beseech Your Majesty to let me go, that I may depart and rejoin my brethren who abide in the wilderness. Do not place obstacles in my way, nor distress yourself unduly. Who knows—perhaps the conclusion of this affair will bring you joy greater than the sorrow which today you suffer on my account. As for the evil which, so you said, has befallen you—such is the nature of evil that it never befalls men when it happens to suit them. The greatest of ills is that for which there is no remedy after death. But when an evil is curable, then we should submit to it, provided that finally normal peace is restored.

'It seems to me that Your Majesty has understood nothing of the extent of my woes, while I am fully conversant with your own. The chief of my miseries is that you do not know Jesus Christ, the Son of God, and have not listened to the voice of His prophets and apostles. Not one of His precepts have you taken in; you have no fear of God, nor have you submitted to His tribunal of righteousness, nor shrunk from exposing me to condemnation. I have no wish to make my own situation publicly known, for I see that your mind is firmly fixed in its refusal to acknowledge God, and I do not wish to cause you travail and grief. It was you who spied upon me, forced me to bandy words with you, and equipped me with boldness to oppose your paternal authority. You tell me that you have voluntarily incurred evil and humiliation for the sake of your love for me and on my behalf. But I fail to see what concessions Your Majesty has made in my favour, or in what way you have changed your previous convictions. You say that you feel tender towards your offspring, as other fathers do. But my impression is that birds, animals and wild beasts feel more tenderness towards their little ones than you do; for they love their young and sacrifice themselves for their sake not because they see in them heirs to themselves, or a support against their enemies, or a boost to their own prestige, but solely from the natural instinct of parenthood.

'It is not for my own good, O king, that you desire me to remain in this worldly life, but for the sake of your own reputation. You must realize this clearly, namely that your censure detracts from the generosity of your gift and diminishes it. The reproaches you heap on my head bring me no benefit; in placing this world at my disposal, you are robbing me of my personal integrity. I should be better pleased if you would acknowledge God, the Creator of all things, the Father invisible, His only-begotten Son Jesus Christ and His most Holy Spirit which shares His dominion equally and has no beginning, indivisible and of essence unmixed, one Deity in three persons, in preference to this whole world, filled though it be with precious stones, but replete even more with sin and all unrighteousness.'

When the king had heard his son's speech, he was more amazed than ever, and loved him still more deeply. He said to Iodasaph: 'My boy! I levelled no reproach at you, nor did I try to coerce you, but only alluded to your opposition and refusal to obey me. Never did any king treat a son of his so generously, nor any man his brother, as I have treated you. For I have handed down my royal estate to you before my own death, permitted you to abandon my religion and permitted any who prefer your creed to join you therein. I merely reminded you of this, without reproaching you. So set off now in accordance with my command, for this will be to my advantage and to yours.'

Iodasaph answered and said to his father: 'It is not surprising that Your Majesty should have acted thus, seeing that you are universally known for your extreme magnanimity and noble conduct. I am not ignorant of your good deeds, nor do I withhold the thanks I owe you. My only wish is that you should crown the favours and goodness which you bestow upon me by excusing me from this undertaking which is uncongenial to my spirit and has no merit in my eyes. Let me rejoin my friends for whom my heart yearns. My soul longs to go out to them swiftly, so that I may not miss the joys which are prepared for their benefit. I have no desire for a transitory kingdom, administered by human adroitness and guile—a kingdom which may exist today, but tomorrow will have faded from our sight.'

Then King Abenes burst into tears and said to Iodasaph his son: 'My child, my child, do not pour scorn upon your parent! Do not rebel against me and revile my royal estate, for I wish to secure your happiness and protect you from shame. Do not drive me beyond the limits of endurance or try to humiliate me for the sake of your own caprice. Do not place obstacles in my way, lest I lose my temper and cancel all the promises I have made you, unleashing upon you my wrath and malediction.'

When the boy Iodasaph heard the king's words, he was afraid that in his anger, his father would lose all self-control, change his mind, and refuse to do what he had promised, so that the concessions which Iodasaph had won would be lost. So from now on Iodasaph began to humour the king in his behaviour, and assumed responsibility for governing the half of his kingdom which had been entrusted to him. But that precious jewel of his—the pure faith of Christ our God—he kept safely and preserved immutably within his mind.

52. When the king observed how his son had yielded, he rejoiced with great joy and ordered a herald to be despatched to summon together the dukes and all the dignitaries of the nation and the entire people. When they had all assembled in his presence, the king ordered a throne just like his own to be set up for his son, and seated him upon it. The king began to speak, saying: 'We all of us once belonged to a different creed and a different religion from that to which we now adhere. All our ancestors, monarchs renowned for their good qualities, and all the nation too used to live according to a different creed from

our present one. But we have given our preference to a religion differing from their original creed, though we have no doubt that had our forebears been alive today, they could not have devised any better body of doctrine for us to adopt now that they are dead.[1] Now all you grandees know about my son's behaviour, in fact news of it has spread throughout the entire people. We have no right to employ coercion against our son because of his opposition to us, seeing that we too rose up in rebellion against the faith of our fathers. So now we have given our consent to the course which he has chosen for himself. Furthermore it is my desire to share with him the use and enjoyment of my kingdom, and to reveal to him the extent of the territory over which he is to reign himself. Whoever wishes to follow him, let him proceed to the prince's domains, for I shall force nobody to remain under my own royal authority. Whoever so wills, let him go wherever he likes and follow whichever religion he prefers. I shall not hinder anyone who wishes to honour and exalt my son, for he is my own child and there is nobody more loyal to me than he is. And now I have given orders to hand over to him one half of everything which is in my store house, both in treasure and in armour, and whatever else is to be found there, so that his reign may be associated with riches, and he may be equipped to mete out fit reward for merit and retribution for deeds of evil.'

When the king had finished this speech, orators arose and glorified his kingly design; and they pledged their obedience to his royal authority and lauded his proposals. Then Iodasaph departed to his own palace, attended by a throng of people giving voice to praise and applause, and a number of them offering their congratulations. After a brief interval, he opened his doors and everybody entered in without fear to listen to his words of wisdom. Among them were certain survivors of the Christian community who had preserved their faith in secret but conformed outwardly to the king's religion from fear of death. When they heard of this event, they rejoiced greatly and ceased to feel any terror. So they came to visit Iodasaph now

---

[1] The author of the Greek recension took this as an allusion to the legendary mission of the Apostle Thomas, who is supposed to have established Christianity in India in the first century A.D. Abenes thus appears as a renegade from the Christian religion. Cf. *Barlaam and Ioasaph*, ed. and trans. Woodward and Mattingly, Loeb Classical Library, 1914, pp. 6-11.

that the young prince was victorious, and felicitated him on the triumph which had been granted to him through the power of Christ Jesus. They told him of their own religious convictions and prepared to depart into Iodasaph's kingdom.

When King Abenes had rendered royal honours to his son and equipped him for the journey into his own domains, Iodasaph arose and went to have a farewell audience with the king. He gave thanks to his father and recalled the blessings which he had bestowed upon him. Then Iodasaph begged him to release all those detained in jail, so that he himself might deal with them as he saw fit. The king gave his consent to his plea, and Iodasaph ordered them to bring out all the prisoners who were detained through failure to pay their taxes to the state. As for those who were imprisoned for debt, he ordered their liabilities to be discharged from his own coffers, and let them go. Concerning those detained for acts of wickedness and murder, the prince ordered that provision should be made for them out of his own resources, sufficient to provide for them amply in prison until God's will might be made known as to what their fate should be. After this he ordered great quantities of treasure to be distributed among the disabled, the poor and the feeble, and finally set off for his own kingdom. And many of the townspeople accompanied him on his journey.

53. When he had arrived in his own realm, he began by thanking God and said: 'Glory to Thee, O God and Father of Our Lord and Liberator Jesus Christ, mighty and omnipotent Deity; I praise and glorify Thee, O Holy Trinity, who dost govern all things with consummate ease.'—And then he began to address the multitude and said: 'No one has a greater duty to walk in justice than a king; and no one is better entitled to address his subjects with words of mildness than a king who goes among his people administering justice with equity. Men should also employ mild words in their dealings with one another. But if there is one placed in authority over the people, a man merciless, bloodthirsty and rapacious, then he too will have recourse to honeyed words whereby to disguise the wickedness of his acts. Again, if some ignorant novice should succeed to the throne, he will use them to conceal his incompetence until he shall have mastered the art of government. But he who diffuses justice

among the people and administers their affairs well, not robbing the honourable of their honour nor the weak of their just deserts, a man who sharpens the sword of justice for the defence of the entire nation—such a one as this has no need to resort to the use of fair words. I for my part have come among you to excel not by my eloquence, but by executing righteous justice.'

After this Iodasaph selected a place of modest appearance, neither a royal palace nor a poor man's cabin, and ordered it to be made ready for his occupation; and he had it furnished in a style neither majestic nor mean, and stored there all the treasure which he had brought with them. Then he came and took up his abode in that place.

54. As for all the regalia which his father had given him—including steeds and garments, decorations for thrones, and many kinds of royal adornments—he ordered all these to be transported to places abroad and sold there, and the proceeds distributed among the poor and destitute and people devoid of resources who were ashamed to go out and beg. Whereas other rulers habitually enjoy life and rejoice in their pomp and abundance of fine raiment and excite the envy of the poor by their pride and arrogance, Iodasaph applied the receipts from the sale of these to comfort the poor and needy. And all people who heard of this glorified Christ our God.

Accordingly Iodasaph ordered letters to be written to every district of his realm—to every province, every canton and every village—with instructions to compile a register of all the poor and needy, the feeble and disabled, and particularly those impoverished people whom shame prevented from begging, and who suffered seven times more than other paupers; and they were all to be entered with their name, that of their village, and the extent of their individual needs. When the register was laid before him, Iodasaph ordered a great quantity of treasure to be distributed among them, to each according to his need, and also grants of land to be made. He helped them to build themselves farms and provided them with the necessary seed corn, until he succeeded in abolishing poverty and misery altogether. Thenceforth everyone became prosperous, for which they glorified God with united voice; and there was not a single man to be found in Iodasaph's domains who needed to go begging for his daily bread or for alms.

Afterwards Iodasaph ordered an announcement to be published throughout his kingdom that each principality or duchy within it should elect for itself a man of upright and worthy character, a doer of righteousness and hater of falsehood. Those who were elected he appointed to be bishops, that they might lead the people to the knowledge of the truth of Christ our God in uprightness and virtue, and sustain and govern their flock with a right judgment.

Then he issued orders to the princes and dukes and officials, that they should judge the people equitably and administer their affairs with mercy and justice, instilling fear into evil doers and imparting peace and joy to the virtuous. All their vassals were to be instructed to cultivate the land and deliver the correct rate of tribute in accordance with their capacities. After this, Iodasaph fitted out his troops completely with everything they needed and nominated generals and dukes to command them—men of worthy, humble and God-fearing character who tried to avoid public office; as for such as sought and strove after authority, these he excluded completely from posts of command.

Again, he ordered all the goodly prelates and priests to be installed with great honours and built churches throughout his land, so that the people might put Christ's precepts into practice according to the words of their pastors. He ordered them to be provided with all necessary facilities and provisions, according to the position occupied by each one of them respectively. And unspeakable joy reigned throughout the land.

Iodasaph himself attended to the nation's affairs without a moment's relaxation. First of all he enquired into people's private lives and how they ordered their spiritual problems, and then into the facts of their material existence. He treated each one of his subjects according to his personal circumstances with both generosity and kindness. He relieved them from fear of royal despotism, and removed from their hearts all apprehension and dread of unfair treatment.

55. Good order, justice and gladness increased among the people, and everybody hastened from all parts to be baptized in the name of the Holy Trinity. Every day countless multitudes

were enrolled into the Christian faith. The superiority of Iodasaph's excellent system became evident, and people began to revile their original religion to which they formerly adhered. All men's hearts were filled with affection for him and with good wishes for the success of his reign. The works and renown of Christianity, of God's service, and of love and peace became manifest to the people, for Iodasaph himself set a shining example to all men of humility, love and devotion to duty. There was nobody left in all his realm serving a different religion from that of God the ruler of all things, except for a few individuals who departed and settled in the kingdom of his father Abenes; these were idolaters who could not bring themselves to adopt the faith of Christ.

Throughout the world there spread the fame of that God-loving young man, of his modesty and patience and ineffable mercy, and how he combined with all these virtues both wisdom and ability. And so there flocked to him from all parts true believers who had been concealing their creed and faith through fear of King Abenes. They settled in security and great happiness within his domains and rejoiced in spirit and glorified the indivisible Holy Trinity, which manifested the unity of its triple essence and revealed the power of the religion of the Christians in face of all the godless. Many former devotees of his father's religion also came and abode with Iodasaph, making public confession of the faith of Christ. Like little children they received baptism in the name of Father, Son and Holy Ghost, and glorified Christ the true God, incarnate without act of human conception of an immaculate virgin who knew no husband, born of His Father before all worlds, having no mother, and sitting upon the throne together with the Father and the Holy Ghost.

56. The renown of the king's son spread abroad. Great was the joy of all the people, and their relief at the cessation of persecution in his father's kingdom. Many were converted and professed the faith of Our Saviour Jesus Christ and the creed of Iodasaph. The preaching of God's word became so intense and ardent among them that the faithful were multiplied and fortified so as to outnumber the godless. Then the influence of Iodasaph's father began to wane and men's hearts were alienated

from him, and people were emboldened to rise in opposition against him. They disregarded many of his ordinances, recalling to mind his immoral behaviour towards them and his tyrannical and cruel actions against them. Popular contempt for King Abenes became daily more apparent, and he realized that men's hearts had turned towards his son. He was afraid that they would rise in revolt against him, and that someone would kill him and seize his kingdom. On this account, he was seized with mighty fear and alarm, which affected not only the king but also all those who were his favourites and counsellors. Consequently they all fell into profound despondency and gloom.

So King Abenes wrote to his son Iodasaph about the situation and told him of all his worries, and asked him what he had better do. Iodasaph wrote back to him as follows: 'Let Your Majesty be informed that there is nothing which dispels fear and removes doubt from the heart of kings more than the exercise of true justice towards the people and sound and merciful administration of their affairs. But there is nothing which induces in a monarch such anxiety, ruins his life, and arouses in him so much distrust towards the people as does unjust treatment of his subjects by the king himself. However much you may multiply your acts of charity towards the people, it takes but the admixture of a little evil to spoil them utterly. Your Majesty provides so clear an example of this situation that there is no longer any need to consult anybody about the problem. You can see for yourself whence come your fears and misgivings, and from what quarter you may look for comfort and hope. My own opinion is that your sole grounds for fear and misgiving arise from the evil deeds which lie behind you, while your only source of comfort and hope is the seeds of good which you have sown. Renounce now all that induces fear and seek out those things which provide tranquillity. Hasten to come to a true decision, lest your enemies outstrip you in the quest for felicity!'

57. When this letter from his son reached the king, he summoned his dignitaries together and read it to them. They began to discuss the problem. Then these men said to the monarch: 'O king, live for ever! We counsel you to get to grips with this crisis directly, before it has dire effects for you. By all means try to remedy those difficulties which will respond to your efforts,

but it is no use resisting pressures which are irresistible. The destiny of a monarchy depends on public opinion, and you are aware that you have treated the people badly. Now you observe how their hearts have turned away from you and their minds become alienated from you. The best counsel one can give a king is to take the right initiative, and the worst, to advise him to wait until events force his hand. Today you have the chance of choosing the most advantageous course to follow and not allowing yourself to be overtaken by the force of circumstances. To act voluntarily is the most honourable way for a king to behave. We would urge you to surrender your entire kingdom to your son, if he will consent to this and will declare his fidelity to you. But to start with, you must summon together all the princes, dukes and dignitaries of your people and concert together with them all necessary steps to achieve this aim.[1] For kings ought not to carry any measure into effect except in a dignified fashion.'

Then the king ordered all the nobles to assemble without delay. When they had gathered in his presence, he began with great deliberation to explain to them the problem at issue. First of all he offered up thanks to God for all His blessings. He went on to refer to his love for the people, and told of how he used to walk among them and watch over their daily wellbeing. Then the king reminded the assembly about how he had lacked a son and feared for the extinction of the royal lineage, and so had promised and made an irrevocable vow to the gods that if a male heir were bestowed upon him, and should he himself survive until the child grew up and was capable of taking over the government of the kingdom, then he, King Abenes, would hand over his entire realm to his son and voluntarily abdicate the kingship, thereby presenting the gods with the thankoffering which he had promised them, and being satisfied from then on to live a simple life as a private citizen.[2]

Then he said to all the people: 'You know how a promise once made must be fulfilled, and a vow must not be broken.

---

[1] Note by the copyist: 'O Christ, have mercy on Michael.'
[2] No previous mention of any such vow by King Abenes is made in our narrative. This story of a vow is doubtless to be regarded simply as a face-saving stratagem, thought up to enable Abenes to abdicate and extricate himself gracefully from an untenable situation.

When I handed over half my kingdom to my son, I imagined that I had carried out my promise. But now I see that its fulfilment is not complete. Since I have been exposed before the gods as a deceiver, I am frightened of the consequences of failing to carry out my promise. They will vent their wrath upon my head, for I have heard that the gods have the right to wreak vengeance on those who fail to fulfil their vows.[1] So now I must make every effort to carry out my promise. I am accordingly consulting you to ask your advice as to what course it will be best for me and for you to follow, so please examine the matter carefully!'

So they replied: 'Who indeed is under a greater obligation to fulfil his vows than a king! And who has always been more punctilious in discharging justice, more steadfast in his discourse, and mightier in his designs than our sovereign!'[2] However, this matter on which you are consulting us raises two different issues. The first relates to the dishonour which a king must incur if he evades or postpones carrying out his obligations. If any man deceives his fellow, he is subject to perpetual condemnation. How much more hateful then is deceit and falsehood committed by a monarch in regard to the gods! What is more, the gods are hardly likely to submit to being cheated by mortals like us. That which you are keen to retain and jealously cling to, they may well take from you in their wrath, without giving you any thanks or even consulting your wishes.

'The second point is that you are handing over your kingdom to your own son, who is the light of your eyes. Quite apart from any vow, all men leave their treasures to their children, thereby fulfilling the hopes they place in them. Had you made a promise in favour of a stranger, it would have been your duty to fulfil it. How much the more then, from both points of view, are you not bound to carry out your obligation towards your own son!

'However, Your Majesty knows that your son abides in the faith of the Christians, whose tenets provide that justice and equality must be conferred upon princes and beggars alike. You know what persecutions we have inflicted upon those men of

[1] Deuteronomy, xxiii. 21: 'When thou shalt vow a vow unto the Lord thy God, thou shalt not slack to pay it: for the Lord thy God will surely require it of thee; and it would be sin in thee.'
[2] Oriental flattery.

repentance. We fear that if their creed gains ground and becomes our official religion, then we may be called to account before the tribunals for the blood which we have shed at your behest, and forced to pay compensation for their estates which we laid waste at your decree.'

58. Then the king wrote to his son in the following terms: 'Peace be to you, my son! You know the ease and luxury in which I brought you up from infancy, and how I then let you follow your own inclination. However grievous the division of my kingdom has been to me, and the convulsions which have taken place in my realm, none the less I have done this out of love for you. Now I want to complete my generosity towards you with favours such as no man has ever conferred on anyone before, and bestow upon you my entire domains. I propose to abdicate my royal estate and retire into private life until my days are accomplished, so that the hopes I placed in you may be fulfilled, and I may witness in my own lifetime the joyous era of your reign.'

King Abenes continued his letter by alluding to those men of repentance—namely the Christians—and the evil which he had done to their persons and their possessions, making the excuse that it is not unknown for kings to act with still greater savagery against their opponents, for the sake of public security. —'Now if you will undertake to mediate with the Christians on behalf of myself and my associates, then I will relinquish the entire kingdom to you, provided that you do not force me and my companions to abandon our own religion.'

Iodasaph wrote to his father the following answer: 'Illustrious crowned head and monarch! You know that no well-ordered realm can tolerate two different systems of law and administration, and that two contrary tendencies cannot exist side by side. With your help, let us put matters on a just basis, such as will do honour to your discernment. I suggest that you send to me a delegation of your own leading men, such as are wise of mind and prudent in judgment so that we may hold discussions with them on this question. From this the truth will emerge, enabling us all to be reconciled on a just footing.'

When the king received his son's letter, he read it out to his associates. They were all pleased with the prince's answer, since they knew that he never did anything that was not strictly just.

59. Then the king selected from among his followers wise men well versed in their own doctrines, and sent them to Iodasaph. When they arrived in the prince's presence, he ordered a like number of selected Christian monks to be summoned, expert in holy writ. And he said to them: 'Do not indulge in long-winded speeches nor place your trust in your own selves, but beseech Christ to grant you power from on high, as it is written in the Holy Gospel where it says: "Do not be anxious what you will speak."'[1]

When the two sides met together, they undertook to conduct their discussion without any element of violence or deviation from the matter in hand, but that they would examine one another's viewpoint with impartiality. This would save the prince from having to use force to quell the rancour of the opposing factions.

When they had undertaken to follow this procedure, the idolaters began by declaring that those seeking to elicit information had the right to pose the first question.—'Before making any enquiries from you,' they continued, 'we will inform you of our own principles. We serve idols of gold and silver and images of stone and wood. Now pray inform us who it is that you serve?'

To this the monks, those servants of Christ our God, replied: 'We serve the life-giving God who created us and also created gold and silver, stones and wood. You know His name, and cannot deny His might. He is chief and supreme over all, and no one can attain to His divine majesty, nor can anyone describe Him in words or see Him with their eyes. He gave us birth and vouchsafed to us knowledge of Himself. We do His will to the best of our ability, and what is distasteful to Him, that we avoid.

'That is our answer to your question. But what are these gods of yours, and what precepts do they teach you? If you are prepared to admit that they have neither created us, nor vouchsafed any body of doctrine to us, and are in fact incapable of creating anything whatever, because they see not, neither do they hear, nor utter any sound with their throats—then in that event you have no case to advance in reply to us, serving as you

---

[1] Matthew, x. 19.

do useless, inanimate objects, which can perform no action, either beneficial or harmful.'

When the idol-worshippers heard this, they were stricken dumb. They could find no words with which to answer the two propositions. For if they claimed that their idols had created them and taught them how they ought to act, then their fraud would be exposed and they would be justly put to shame by their adversaries' wise words. But if they admitted that their idols were powerless and unable to create anything or perform any action either beneficial or harmful, then they would be deservedly vanquished, and their opponents' cause would triumph. Since they could find no other solution to help them out, they conceded the superiority of the faith and creed of Christ our God over every other religion on earth. For they observed the great virtues of Iodasaph's exemplary conduct and his exceeding humility and mercy, as a result of which great peace and joy prevailed within his kingdom.

So the idolaters answered and said: 'O king's son, what will be your verdict concerning us in regard to those previous acts which we performed at the orders of your father our sovereign, and the blood which we spilt in our ignorance?'

The blessed Iodasaph said to them: 'As soon as you shed your religion, you may shed simultaneously any misgivings you entertain on that score. As soon as you enter into the religion of our God and Saviour Jesus Christ, you will enter immediately into the realm of peace and joy, for He is the God of peace and love, and not of spite and rancour.'

Afterwards those men returned into the presence of King Abenes and informed him of everything which they had heard and seen. Then the king and all his people decided to follow the faith of Iodasaph. And they accepted holy baptism in the name of the Father, the Son and the Holy Ghost. The only exception was that anchorite named Thedma whom we have mentioned previously—the man who advised the king to combat his son by the devil's agency; and this person still refused to adopt the Christian faith.

60. The king and all his people wrote a joint epistle to the prince, declaring that they confessed and believed in the Father, the Son and the Holy Ghost. When the envoys reached

Iodasaph, and told him of the decision of the king and the entire people, he was filled with exceeding great joy; and he arose and lifted his arms aloft towards heaven and offered up thanks to Christ, who fulfils the desires of those that fear Him. And he treated the envoys with honour, presented them with generous gifts and let them go without delay.

And Iodasaph wrote a letter to his father in the following terms: 'To the great and pious king, fortunately entered into God's allegiance: I the slave and wretch Iodasaph greet you in the Lord's name! First I thank Christ, the Son of God, who was made man for the salvation of mankind and saved us from servitude and the trickery of idols and redeemed us with His innocent and illustrious blood, which He shed upon the Cross. I praise and glorify the grace of Him who looked down upon me with mercy and has not deprived me of my desire, and has made me worthy to look upon your veritable royalty: for now indeed you have become a king, whereas previously you were accounted lower than a slave. Great are your favours towards me, and I cannot sufficiently thank you for everything which you have done for me. But greatest of all is the joy which you have brought me at this time. For everything which you had previously bestowed upon me was as nothing before my eyes. But now that you have attained knowledge of the truth, the Holy Trinity will be exalted and the religion thereof will shine forth more brightly, now that you have adopted it for your own.

'At present you must place your relations with me on an even loftier footing. You must know that no man can really give up one of his friends until he has overcome the long-standing habits of old acquaintance. A man's conversion must likewise be considered dubious until the basic cause of his deviation from the truth has been thoroughly rooted out. The veracity of your words and the purging of your heart in the sight of God, whereby you plan to join with us in serving God and in prayerful communion, can only be made manifest if you destroy the temples of the idols and burn the images with fire for God's sake, so that retribution may be meted out to them for the harm they have done to countless nations. By burning them you will reconcile yourself with God, just as previously you alienated the Deity against you by burning His saints. When you have done this, you will have torn down the barrier wall of enmity and can receive true and immutable comfort from God the giver of life, and from us, His slaves.'

When King Abenes received this letter and it was read out to him, he arose immediately and all his people with him, and they began to destroy and burn the idols and the shrines of the images, until the very site they had occupied was no longer to be seen. After this the king went forth with all his people to the kingdom of Iodasaph his son and surrendered to him his entire realm, all except Thedma the hermit, who was tormented with redoubled anguish, but still refused to be converted.

When Iodasaph learnt that the king and all his subjects were approaching, he arose and went out to meet them with great joy; and he fell down before Abenes together with all the multitude of Christian believers who had come out with Iodasaph to greet the king. Abenes embraced Iodasaph's neck with great affection and kissed him with tears in his eyes. And Iodasaph escorted his father with exceeding great honour and entertained him with all that pomp and circumstance which he himself had renounced.

61. One day when Iodasaph was sitting in his father's presence, Thedma made his way into their company, bursting with rage and intent on provoking Iodasaph into a dispute about religion. So he said to him: 'Tell me, O prince, why you have done this thing? What harm have the idols done to you that you should treat them with such spite? Did they not once upon a time exalt your forefathers to be kings? Did they not elevate your father, King Abenes, in regal glory and raise him up higher than any other monarch on this earth, as well as driving from his heart the pang of childlessness? All the thanks you gave them for this was to abandon your faith and betray your father! Why have you cut yourself off from serving your gods by this apostasy of yours, as well as alienating your father from them, and falsifying the hopes and insulting the memory of all the god-fearing monarchs your ancestors?'

King Iodasaph answered and said: 'Listen to me, O utterer of falsehood and foe of truth, who have embraced the wisdom of this world in all its lunacy, but spurned the supreme wisdom, which is the fear of the Lord! You imagine yourself to be wise but are besotted, because those idols which you serve are objects of gold and silver and brass, or carved from stone and wood, and they can bring no benefit to us or anybody else, nor any harm either. How could they be capable of anything, seeing that they are themselves dead? They hear not neither do they see, nor do they possess any knowledge. Rouse yourself up from your dream, if there be any vestige of life left in you! This world is transitory, as are we men and all the animals and birds, and the trees and the various kinds of fruit they bring forth, which ripen at different seasons for men's enjoyment. All this is from Almighty God, with whom no other deity can compare, nor is there any other creed like His; and He created us by His almighty power, that we might glorify Him.

'God gave us all beautiful things for our delight, so that whenever we behold these good and pleasant things we may believe also in that bliss eternal which the eye has not seen, the ear has not heard of, nor has the heart any glimmer of perception thereof, but which He has prepared for His faithful servants. We are assured of this by the prophets, His elected servants, and by the glorious apostles. God did not create these delights for our mere amusement, or to distract us from obeying His commandments, but for us to derive benefit from them in moderation. Thus they should help us to be more diligent in serving Him and not captivate our hearts to such an extent that we neglect His precepts. If on the other hand this world's gifts are spread out before mankind solely for them to eat, drink and enjoy themselves with, while hoping to prolong their sojourn therein, then I must say that your idols have given you a pretty small share in the world's goods—in fact nothing but those tatters which you have wound round your middle and the staff which is in your hand. You are satisfied with this transitory world which you praise and put your trust in, but you have nothing satisfactory to show for it. If it is good to set one's hopes on this material world, then why do you make no effort to improve your own lot? But if these delights were created in order to arouse desire in us for that eternal bliss, to confirm our faith and provide us with provisions for the way to Heaven, so that we may arrive safely in the abode of our Creator and our God, then it is clear that your belief is misguided. For you do not even know why you are tormenting yourself, whither you are bound, or from whom you can expect to receive recompense for your labours, seeing that you neither place your hope in the hereafter, nor derive any enjoyment from life in this world below!'

When Thedma had heard these words of Iodasaph's, he was silent for a long time as he meditated over what King Iodasaph had said, but he could find no answer to give. At length he replied and said to him: 'You have pierced my heart with these words of yours, for they have stabbed my soul like a sword. Now I should like you to incline your ears to listen to me and discuss this question more explicitly.'

King Iodasaph said: 'Behold, I am ready to listen to you and apply my mind to debate the question with you. So ask now whatever you like.'

Thedma answered and said: 'If those idols we serve are not gods, then who is this god of yours?'

Iodasaph said to him: 'My God is the Father of My Lord Jesus Christ, the Creator of heaven and earth and of all things that exist therein, both spiritual and corporeal.'

Thedma said: 'How do you know that heaven and earth have ever been created?'

Iodasaph said to him: 'I know this because there are signs and symbols of their origin which witness to the fact of their creation, and this is intelligible to the human reason. They must logically be either combined or separate, either mobile or stationary, and we observe that all created things tend towards unity or isolation, motion or tranquillity. Hence I know that heaven and earth are of the same nature as created beings; nor can they add anything to the glory of the rest of creation.'

Thedma said: 'How can you confirm the testimony of the apostles and the prophets, seeing that you have never set eyes on them?'

Iodasaph said to him: 'I can confirm it by the fact that everywhere, in lands far separated from one another, their testimony has been accepted, even by kings of differing creeds who were at enmity with one another, and between whom no agreement existed. Although I have not set eyes on the apostles and the prophets, I know of them from incessant reports which cannot be discounted and wherein there can be no conspiracy to deceive; for they emanate from remote places, and in the east and the west, the south and the north, glory is offered up to the Father, the Son and the Holy Spirit and their sacred law which God's holy and elect apostles preached. How could there have been any prearranged collusion between all these witnesses?'

Thedma answered and said: 'How do you know that the prophets speak the truth, and that they are really sent by God?'

King Iodasaph declared: 'I know that they speak the truth because they have shown the world signs and miracles such as no mortal man could possibly effect. These miracles were performed by divine power, so that the world might believe, and all men might know that their faith is true, and that the prophets are the chosen of God among all nations.'

Thedma continued to enquire and ask questions of Iodasaph in his father's presence. Finally Thedma himself was brought to acknowledge and believe in Our Lord Jesus Christ, an inner voice prompting him and saying: 'Iodasaph speaks the truth, and you are performing a vain task in worshipping the idols.' Then Thedma made his confession aloud, saying: 'There is no god on earth apart from the Father supreme and his only-begotten Son and the most holy Spirit, being conjoint in essence, God in three persons and of one substance, Creator of heaven and earth.' And he accepted the entire Christian creed and believed, and he accepted holy baptism, and from then onwards began to observe the commandments of Christ and steadfastly offered up prayers to God and glorified His name.

62. King Abenes persevered mightily in the righteous conduct which he had adopted from his son, and made fitting public atonement for his previous crimes. But when his death drew near, he became very frightened and quaked with dread, and great alarm overcame him.

Then Iodasaph said to him: 'My father! Why are you terrified on account of this worldly life? If you were hoping to remain on this earth for ever, then surely you realize that no man can achieve this. Is it that you wish to attain to the extreme limit of old age, when you would be afflicted with many hideous infirmities, your head and hands would tremble, and you would have lost all the appetites that make life worth living? Or do you imagine that you can be restored afresh to youthful vigour with your life ahead of you, in addition to the lifespan which you have already enjoyed? This also is beyond men's powers to achieve. Or are you wavering in your trust in the Lord's mercies, and reluctant to respond to His summons? Thereby you will draw divine wrath down upon your head! It is your duty now to accept with gratitude the call which you have received from God, since you have known from the very first that you are but a mortal creature within this world, just as all your ancestors before you were mortal.'

King Abenes answered and said to Iodasaph: 'No, my son, it is not for this reason that my spirit is downcast, as you allege; but it is inherent by nature in every soul to feel grief at quitting the flesh, leaving the air and the light, and departing to a strange and narrow place. I know not what ordeals my soul will encounter there, because I have greatly angered God my Maker, and have despatched many of my adversaries before me into the world beyond, and these will now urge God to wreak vengeance upon me. All the days of my life I have cursed God and praised idols. I have neither propitiated my Judge nor disarmed my accuser. From where shall I receive support when I stand in Christ's presence? Even the time of my repentance has been cut short, so that I have not succeeded in making fit atonement to God.'

The blessed Iodasaph answered and said to his father: 'Have no care, O king, but be glad, because you are going before a gracious and much forgiving Sovereign, who grants even those of the eleventh hour the same reward as those of the first.[1] He will accept this gesture of reconciliation which you offer at the very end of your life, for God's mercies are deficient in nothing; neither does the Lord judge according to the way of men, for his compassion outweighs all the wickedness of this sinful world. Do not belittle God's mercy; for the Lord's purposes are not as those of men. What is more, the light of this world and its air so highly desired by men cannot compare with the light of His face and the air of His glory, of which the faithful shall be made worthy after they have drunk this draught which you are terrified to taste. No one may put on the imperishable raiment until he has endured the perishing of the flesh. A righteous man considers this mortal life to be just as cramped in comparison with the life hereafter as might a babe emerging from the confinement of the womb and catching sight of the broad expanse and

---

[1] Cf. Matthew, xx. 1-16.

brightness of the world. Fret not, nor say that your repentance is but slight compared with the grievous sins you have committed in God's sight. For in God's eyes, a little repentance wipes out a multitude of great sins, because He lavishes His mercies and multiplies their fruit, and the soul shall rejoice therein mightily.'

At this, King Abenes regained his courage and rejoiced at his son's words, and was relieved of his anxiety. And he said to Iodasaph: 'May God of His bounty grant you the supreme reward, my son, even exceeding the bounds of your hopes. For I was lost and you found me, doomed and you saved me, an enemy of God and you reconciled me with Him, a corpse and you revived me. Now I exhort you, my son, to walk virtuously before God and complete your days in fear of Him; let not the pomp of kingship turn you away from the love of Christ, for all visible creation is but shadowy and transitory, but you should always seek out what is invisible. Behold now—where is the terror of my own majesty, the multitude of my hosts, the courage of my valiant knights, or my countless treasures which I heaped up for myself? How shall they come and deliver me today from death as it is about to bear me off? Now it is my turn to exhort you, my son, just as you have previously exhorted me; and I admonish you, just as you have admonished me, to despise the world and all its glory, and seek only after God. For He is superior to this world with all its abundance. But cause me to be remembered in your prayers, O my son!'[1]
—And when King Abenes had pronounced these words, he cried out with a loud voice and delivered up his spirit.

63. Iodasaph bore away his body and laid it to rest in company with the remains of other pious believers, not with regal pomp, but in the simple grave of a common man. Then Iodasaph raised his hands aloft and directed his gaze towards Heaven and said: 'I praise and thank Thee, O God and Father of My Lord and Saviour Jesus Christ, O King of Glory, great and mighty, unattainable and unknowable, invisible and indescribable and infinite, Creator of all things, who didst not make my soul desolate but didst convert this errant slave of Thine, who came to

---

[1] Note by the scribe: 'Pray for the very sinful David!'

know you at the last moment as God supreme, and confessed Thy Son, born before all ages, and Thy most Holy Ghost; and Thou didst cause him to believe in Thy Holy Trinity. Make him worthy to behold the light of Thy face and enter the abode of peace in Thy kingdom in company with all Thy saints who have carried out Thy will! Remember not his earlier crimes, but by Thy mercy and manifold grace forgive him his sins and relieve him of the weight of guilt which oppresses him as a result of his previous godlessness; deliver him from the wrath of the saints and chosen servants of Thine whom he despatched with fire and the sword! For Thou art omnipotent and all things are possible to Thee, except that Thou art incapable of lacking mercy towards those who offer prayers of remorse to Thee with tears and sighs.'

These and many such supplications on his father's behalf did Iodasaph offer up to God with tears in his eyes. Then he fell on his face and laid his hands on his father's grave and said: 'O Christ my God, who didst create my father before me and didst grant me to be born of his loins and didst vouchsafe to me the pleasure of living with him for as long as it was Thy will, and then didst afflict me by parting me from him when Thou didst decree it! Abide by him as his comforter, O Lord, in the strange world of eternity and be my Protector and Saviour too when my own turn comes! Show me the way to salvation according to Thy will, for Thou art gracious and beneficent!'—He remained there at the tomb until the seventh day, praying for his father. And then he laid unsparing hands upon his treasures and distributed them to the poor, the feeble and the sick.

64. On the eighth day Iodasaph appeared and took his seat before the people according to his custom, and all his grandees with him; and he said: 'Behold, King Abenes my father has found rest, just like any ordinary mortal from among the poorer classes, and no one could help him and save him, neither I myself nor any of you; and this day of reckoning must come upon each one of us also. You know what was my personal desire from the very first: however I was powerless to resist my father. But now I no longer have any excuse before God for not fulfilling my promise to join the number of the monks and adhere strictly to their way of life. So do you choose for yourselves a

king to guide you in the will of God. Today by God's grace no adversary of truth remains, and this you all know full well.'

But when the people heard this, they all arose and cried out with a loud voice: 'Let this not be, O king, and let our ears never hear such words again. Rather let us perish than that this should come to pass!' Whereupon their voices grew louder and louder, until their shouts produced a regular tumult within the city.

Seeing that they refused to consent, Iodasaph determined to get away secretly by means of a ruse. So he summoned that man who, as we mentioned earlier, was prepared to support Balahvar on the occasion of the debate arranged by the king with Nakhor, Balahvar's double. This person was a kinsman of their royal house, and his name Barakhia.

Iodasaph said to Barakhia: 'Every man has need of the help of another in the day of trouble. You are my kinsman, and I will confide my secret in you and also entrust you with a great undertaking, if it be the Lord's will. Accept now this charter addressed by me to the people and to my princes concerning your accession to the throne, and I shall depart and join my brethren and serve Christ my God in their company. If you refuse to perform this service for me, then you will cease to be any kinsman of mine.'

Barakhia answered and said to him: 'You have not made a fair decision, O king, for it is written: "Love thy neighbour as thyself."[1] But you have chosen for yourself the better thing, and intend to ruin me. If regal estate be a blessing, then why do you not go on reigning? For just as a child weeps for its absent mother, so all your subjects are crying out for you to stay by them. But if it is preferable to quit the transitory world and seek after the eternal, why are you choosing this course for yourself and casting me into perdition? Do you wish to encompass your own salvation through my damnation? Rather let us both arise and depart together!'

65. When Iodasaph had listened to Barakhia's words, he realized the justice of his objections and made no answer to him. But one night he arose and left the palace, leaving behind on his

---

[1] Matthew, xix. 19.

couch a charter addressed to the people, declaring: 'Barakhia deserves to be king—set him upon the throne!' This he did in order to avoid any popular upheaval over the succession to the crown.

Barakhia had already suspected what Iodasaph intended to do, seeing that the king returned no answer to his words. So he went forth and gathered together the princes and counsellors and told them what Iodasaph had said, warning them that the king had been planning to go away secretly. At this they arose in haste and pursued him by various routes. They found the blessed Iodasaph in a valley, holding up his arms aloft in the form of a cross and praying to God. When he saw them approaching, he said to them: 'Why are you making all this commotion? From now on I am no longer your king!'

By their weeping, those men obliged Iodasaph to return against his will; and they inundated his feet with tears. When they brought him to their city, the entire nation assembled, from the highest to the lowest, including women and children; and they surrounded him and besought him, weeping and crying out: 'God will hold you to account for our blood. If you do not remain with us, then we shall raise up the idols once more, and you will be responsible in God's eyes.'

But Iodasaph said to them: 'Christ, who delivered you from the blindness of ignorance and showed you the true light of the knowledge of God, will Himself fortify your belief. I have already shown you what you must do, and you have received my teaching and eaten of the fruit of my labours. Henceforth I have no further obligation towards you for, according to the words of Saint Paul the Apostle, "I have finished the course",[1] and now I must look to my own salvation. And the discussion continued until the seventh day. Then Iodasaph uttered a vow that he would not remain there any longer, but would depart into the wilderness.

When the people heard him utter this vow, they realized that they could not shake his resolve; for they knew his strength of will once he had decided on a course of action. Then they all came to Iodasaph with tears in their eyes and fell at his feet and embraced them and asked him about the future of the

---

[1] II Timothy, iv. 7.

monarchy. And he said to them: 'Barakhia deserves to be your king.'

But Barakhia began to weep and refused to consent. However he was powerless to prevail against the people and most of all, against Iodasaph himself. Then Iodasaph took the royal signet ring and placed it upon Barakhia's hand; and he raised his eyes towards heaven in the presence of all the people, and said: 'O Lord Jesus Christ, who didst come down from the bosom of the Father without being parted from Him, and wast made man for us men, and didst take on mankind's servile state from a maiden not yet wed, and deliver mankind from servitude to the devil—I praise and glorify Thee, O Lord and lover of men, because Thou hast saved me, Thine unworthy slave, and granted me the faculty of knowing Thee; and Thou hast filled my soul with joy through the conversion of my father and given me strength to glorify Thy holy name. Now make manifest again Thy benevolence, and help Barakhia, this brother of mine, that he may walk before Thee in a worthy and virtuous manner, and conduct himself before the face of the entire nation in accordance with his love for Thee.'

He addressed many such supplications to God, with his hands laid upon Barakhia's shoulders. Then he turned to Barakhia and said: 'Behold I give you this exhortation and testament, O Barakhia, in the presence of God and of the entire nation. Let me not be exposed to blame through any conduct of yours. Just as you knew God before I did and served Him with a quiet spirit, strive now more zealously than I myself to make your perfect virtue manifest to God. Harbour no malice against anyone. Direct your speech solely towards the furtherance of God's purposes. Follow not the vicissitudes of the times, nor promote schism within the faith of Christ; do not let your intellect be put out of joint by the pomp of your throne. Set not your hopes upon any other helper but God alone. Do not be puffed up if God satisfies your ambitions; do not stretch out your hand with intent to snatch some delight which does not belong to you. Faint not in furthering God's purpose, nor deliver any verdict not in accordance with equity. Accept no corrupt gifts in return for false testimony. Deliver even the unrighteous if any appeal to you because of the heavy weight of their yoke. Do not subject your reason to the dictates of your flesh, nor leave your tongue without a curb. Do not rejoice at a foe's discomfiture, however evil he may be. Let not your mind be inflamed in moments of anger nor look upon anyone with guileful eyes, nor harbour dislike of anyone without just cause. Do not inflict vengeance on anyone of your own account, but only for the sake of vindicating God's cause. Turn the poor not away empty from your gate, nor abandon anyone whose mind thirsts for the divine message.—These precepts I give you in the sight of God, and if you observe them, you shall live; if you reject them, God will hold you to account for breaking your vow. However, you may trust God, that He will not demand from you anything which exceeds your powers.'

And then Iodasaph added: 'May Our Lord God Jesus Christ be the beginning and the end of all your deeds.—Test out everything and choose what is best. Poverty which is not endured with patience is a bad thing, but still worse is wealth allied to arrogance. Seek goodness from God, for He is the mainspring of every virtue. Put a curb on your flesh and tremble with fear before God. Bridle your lust, so that you may not lose your mental balance. Let your wisdom be tempered by reason, that you succumb not to conceit; may your learning serve you as a lantern throughout life, and do not imagine yourself to be other than you are. Examine every alternative, and do what is correct. Look upon yourself as a wanderer, and cherish all those that wander. Draw nigh to the abode of those that fear God and shun the abode of the unrighteous. Do not gloat over a friend's discomfiture, lest you turn him into a rival who will one day laugh you to scorn. Be prepared to sacrifice yourself even unto death for God's sake. If you observe these rules, you shall bring salvation to yourself and your people. Offer your observance of them as a spiritual sacrifice to God, and Christ himself will watch over and direct your doings.

'If you are certain that you are without sin in God's eyes, then you need not forgive other men their sins; if however you know that you must yourself be judged, then you yourself should extend forgiveness to others. Like some merchant generous in his dealings, send on your oblations in advance, for God will repay charity with charity. To nobody will more be given than he has the capacity to appreciate. What treasure can you lay up for yourself more precious than charity! Therefore give to the poor their fair share.

'Let this world be your stock in trade; and if you dispose thereof, you yourself will be the gainer. For you will be giving away little and winning far more; you will lose what is transitory and acquire what is eternal. If you fail to exert yourself here below, your stock in trade will vanish away. Better a glut of goodness than a famine of it!

'Be exalted in intelligence and not in lust, for the former lifts a man up towards God, and the latter hurls him down into the abyss. One who deems himself perfect is none the less far below the level of Christ's precepts. It is better to listen to improper language than to utter it oneself. Do not count on the peaceful completion of your ship's voyage until you reach port; for many a sailor's craft has foundered in a calm sea, while many others have fortunately escaped the pounding of heavy waves and the terror of the hurricanes. Do not display excess of either fortitude or despair.

'Sell all your worldly belongings, and purchase for yourself Jesus Christ free of charge. For your possessions belong to you but a short time. If you find it hard to give away everything, then part with a portion of them. Rob the moth and the thief of their booty and thereby place God in your debt, for He will repay you with interest. In rags and tatters you will win God's approval. Nobody is more sincere than a beggar, for he has no possessions other than his God; therefore purchase his favour by giving him alms. Be not ashamed if anyone calls you "Son of a rascal", but only if someone calls you a rascal yourself. It is more important for a man to be virtuous himself than for him to be the son of a virtuous man, but himself a rascal. That is a curse indeed!

'Act towards every man and every nation as you would wish them to act towards you. Beware of false friends; for a true friend is one whom not the wine-cup but the test of time attaches to you, and who will not speak merely to please you, but rather to benefit both your soul and your subjects. Such a friend is of inestimable worth, so that the love you bear him in your heart should never be exhausted, for it has been stated: "Render therefore to all their dues: tribute to whom tribute is due; custom to whom custom; fear to whom fear; honour to whom honour."[1] Love has no boundary. One eye has need of the other, for it can see everything, but itself it cannot see; likewise one hand needs the help of the other, and one foot that of the other.

'In the same way, a king has need of a reliable counsellor. Subject every problem to careful trial, just as I was tried out by Balahvar. He gave me no guidance on earthly matters, but through the medium of spiritual guidance enabled me to manage even earthly affairs through God's grace, as you can see for yourself. Likewise I give you first of all my spiritual testament, and only then hand over my earthly burden. If the devil tempts you to commit sin, say within your mind: "Everyone will get to know this!" Then you should feel shame at your own self. For nobody can waver from the path of righteousness except one who is spiritually sick through forgetfulness of God. So long as the sins a man commits are curable, he can be restored to health by the art of the physicians and cured by divine grace. When the disease has become more powerful than the remedy, the offending limb must be cut off and thrown away, lest it infect the whole body and do mortal injury to the soul.

'Every feeble and afflicted spirit, if it have little faith in God, is liable to fall into despondency and succumb to sinful impulses. Likewise a worm cannot gnaw through a strong tree, but only a soft and tender sapling. Everyone who yearns for the bliss to come despises this fleshly existence, as confinement within a narrow prison cell. We cannot aspire to receive God's gifts if we do not first purify ourselves; for no one pours fragrant essences and precious myrrh into a filthy pot. True fasting consists in abstinence from all evil, in keeping control over the tongue, restraining one's temper, moderating the lusts, refraining from tale-bearing, lies and taking God's name in vain, and avoiding all forms of sin, bearing in mind that to overcome the desires of the flesh only in extreme old age is no longer counted as a virtue. Nor is it praiseworthy to counteract evil, not by self-control, but solely through a plethora of good works. A righteous judge should resemble an archer who does not bend his bow too far, lest the arrow overshoot the mark, nor too little, lest it fail to reach the target; nor does he shoot his arrow

---

[1] Romans, xiii. 7.

askew, lest it miss the mark altogether. On the contrary, he acts with just moderation and aims straight, so as to hit the centre of the target.

'We know from books that this world has been termed a sea, because the vicissitudes of life in it resemble the ocean billows. Treasures and wealth are insecure, as is even poverty itself. Both of them are eternally within a hair's breadth of shipwreck; just as the sea changes in an instant from tranquil calm to stormy waves, and then reverts to calm again, so it is with the affairs of this world. Therefore you should be like a prudent sailor who does not trust the calm of the ocean, nor loses his grip and his self-confidence when the tempest bursts upon him.

'This is my parting message to you. And I pray to God for your sake and commend you to His mercy. May the God of peace, the Father of Our Lord Jesus Christ, grant you to follow His will, and may the Holy Spirit be your guide and teacher, for to the Holy Trinity belongs glory for ever and ever, Amen.'

66. When the thrice blessed Iodasaph had completed this discourse, he went out in haste and girt himself with the old garment which he had received from Balahvar. And the people followed after him until nightfall, like sheep bereft of their shepherd, and sobbed bitterly with a loud voice, like children mourning for their father.

And the blessed Iodasaph departed into the land of Sarandib in search of the holy Balahvar. After a two years' search, he found him dwelling in the mountains, still wearing the hair apron which Iodasaph had presented to him. When Balahvar caught sight of him, he came forth to meet him and they embraced each other and kissed one another with tears in their eyes and glorified God with great joy. And Balahvar enquired about what had befallen Iodasaph in the meantime. So the blessed Iodasaph told him everything which had happened right up to the last. And they gave thanks to God the three in one, glorified in one substance, who had granted to them both so great a victory, whereby they had won salvation for themselves and for countless other souls.[1]

67. After a few days had passed, the blessed Balahvar's end

[1] Note by the copyist: 'Christ have mercy on the souls of Michael and David, Amen.'

drew nigh. When Iodasaph saw that Balahvar's death was at hand, he began to wail and bemoan and despair took hold of him. And he said to his mentor: 'O father Balahvar, you have not given full effect to your love towards me! For you are departing to enjoy repose from the woes of this world, and leaving me all alone in great grief in a strange land. I know not how I am to live after you are gone, for although you have told me how to order my life, I have not had time to gain practical experience from you. Nor have I any desire to carry on living after you are dead.'

The most blessed Saint Balahvar answered and said: 'Fear not, Iodasaph, for Christ our God is your helper! Sorrow not at my parting but be glad, for I have been delivered from future sins.

'Be glad, Iodasaph, for you have disposed of the earth and acquired the heavens!

'Be glad, Iodasaph, for you have become worthy of apostolic grace!

'Be glad, Iodasaph, for you have won many crowns of witness and of travail through your labours and feats of endurance!

'Do not be downcast at this moment when you are harvesting and eating the crop which you have planted. Place your trust in God who will comfort you and not prevent you from seeing me again soon.' (By this last remark Balahvar was giving Iodasaph to understand that his own death was also nigh.)

Then the holy father Balahvar passed away and entered into the presence of Christ. Iodasaph laid his corpse, emaciated by monastic austerities undergone for Christ's sake, in the grotto carved out in the rock wherein he used to dwell. And he sank into deep sorrow. From the excess of his grief he fell asleep, and saw in a dream certain men radiant with light coming towards him, and having a great quantity of crowns adorned with garnet stones and precious gems without number. But one of them had two crowns glittering more brightly than the others, being more brilliant even than the sun's orb. And they said: 'These are for you, Iodasaph, because of the many souls which you have turned towards God.'

Now the man who bore the two crowns said: 'One of these is for you, Iodasaph, because of the great feats which you have accomplished, and the other is for your father, seeing that he has been converted and turned to repentance.'

Iodasaph was offended at this and retorted: 'What comparison can there be between one who has merely repented, and one who has striven hard?'

Then Balahvar appeared to him and said: 'Remember, O king's son, what I once told you.—For now that you have verily become rich, you are miserly with this treasure of yours, and grudge it even to your own father!'[1]

When Iodasaph awoke from his slumber, he was fortified in spirit.

68. After some little time Iodasaph too passed away, and entered before Christ's presence borne on the wings of the spirit. And a certain holy man dwelling nearby came and laid Iodasaph's corpse by the body of Balahvar. Then he went to the land of Sholait and told King Barakhia everything which he had seen.

The king arose with a great multitude and came to that place together with his princes and bore away the bodies of both the saints, and enclosed them within urns adorned with gold. And Barakhia laid these relics within a hallowed church dedicated to the worship of the Holy Trinity, and exalted them with every mark of honour. Many who were rendered infirm by grievous ailments were delivered from them by these relics, which constantly wrought miracles. And the king and all the people saw this and glorified Christ our God, who readily grants success in all things to those who love Him; for to Him belong glory and honour, grace and adoration together with the Father who has no beginning and the Holy Spirit, giver of life, now and always and for all eternity, Amen.[2]

---

[1] This refers to Balahvar's remarks in Chapter 36, above: ' . . . But I hope that if the Lord wills it, you too will become passing rich and that your fruits and your treasures may be multiplied. But then you too will become miserly, and not so ready to distribute them to all and sundry!'

[2] Here follows in the manuscript a concluding note by the scribe: 'O lovers of Christ, whichever of you light upon this sacred book, pray for the greatly sinful David, that God may forgive him his sins, Amen.'

SELECT BIBLIOGRAPHY AND NOTES FOR FURTHER READING

Note: Since the Romance of Barlaam and Josaphat makes its appearance in most of the languages of mediaeval Christendom, a substantial number of books and articles have been devoted to it. Many of these are listed in the Catalogue of the British Museum, under the rubric: BARLAAM, *Saint, of India*. Professor H. Peri's important study of the Barlaam legend, published at Salamanca in 1959, contains a bibliography of 378 items, while a further selection is given in D. M. Lang, *The Wisdom of Balahvar*, 1957, pp. 125-8. The list given below, which is selective, should be used in conjunction with these publications.

ABULADZE, Bidzina, trans. *Balavariani*. Mudrost' Balavara. ('Balavariani. The Wisdom of Balavar', Russian version, with a preface by I. V. Abuladze.) Tbilisi, 1962.

ABULADZE, Ilia V., edit. 'Balavarianis k'art'uli redak'tsiebi. ('Georgian redactions of Balavariani'), Tbilisi, 1957. (*Dzveli k'art'uli enis dzeglebi*, no. 10.)

——'K'art'uli "Balavarianis" ert'i personazhis sakhelis dsarmomavlobisat'vis.' ('Concerning the formation of the name of a personage in the Georgian "Balavariani" '), in *Moambe* ('Bulletin') of the Academy of Sciences of the Georgian SSR, vol. XXVIII, no. 4, 1962, pp. 511-13.

AŚVAGHOSA. *The Buddhacarita, or, Acts of the Buddha*, edit. and trans. by E. H. Johnston, 2 vols., Calcutta, 1935-6.

——'The Buddha's Mission and Last Journey', in *Acta Orientalia*, vol. XV, Leiden, 1937.

BUDGE, Sir Ernest Wallis, edit. and trans. *Baralâm and Yewâsef* (Ethiopic text and trans.), 2 vols., Cambridge, 1923.

BURKITT, F. C. *The Religion of the Manichees*, Cambridge, 1925.

DER NERSESSIAN, S. *L'Illustration du Roman de Barlaam et Joasaph*, Paris, 1937.

DEVOS, P. 'Les origines du "Barlaam et Joasaph" grec. A propos de la thèse nouvelle de M. Nucubidze', in *Analecta Bollandiana*, LXXV, fasc. 1-2, Bruxelles, 1957, pp. 83-104.

DÖLGER, Franz. *Der griechische Barlaam-Roman, ein Werk des H. Johannes von Damaskos*, Ettal, 1953.

FRANCIS, H. T. and E. J. THOMAS. *Jātaka Tales*, Cambridge, 1916.
HARRIS, J. Rendel and J. Armitage ROBINSON. *The Apology of Aristides*, Cambridge, 1891. (*Texts and Studies*, vol. 1, no. 1.)
HENNING, W. B. 'Persian Poetical Manuscripts from the Time of Rūdakī', in *A Locust's Leg: Studies in honour of S. H. Taqizadeh*, London, 1962, pp. 89-98.
JGHAMAIA, Ts. 'Iodasap'is sagaloblis akhali varianti' ('A new variant of the hymn to Iodasaph'), in *Khelnadsert'a institutis moambe* ('Bulletin of the Institute of Manuscripts'), III, Tbilisi, 1961, pp. 35-57.
JONES, J. J., trans. *The Mahāvastu*, 3 vols., London, 1949-56. (*Sacred Books of the Buddhists*.)
KEKELIDZE, K. S. 'Balavaris romani k'ristianul mdserlobashi' ('The Balavar romance in Christian literature'), reprinted in *Etiudebi dzveli k'art'uli literaturis istoriidan* ('Studies in the history of Ancient Georgian literature'), vol. VI, Tbilisi, 1960, pp. 41-71.
LANG, D. M. Article 'Bilawhar wa-Yūdāsaf' in *Encyclopaedia of Islam*, new edition, pp. 1215-17.
——*The Life of the Blessed Iodasaph*: A New Oriental Christian Version of the Barlaam and Ioasaph Romance, in *Bulletin of the School of Oriental and African Studies*, London, XX, 1957, pp. 389-407.
——*The Wisdom of Balahvar*. A Christian Legend of the Buddha, London, Allen & Unwin, New York, Macmillan, 1957. (*Ethical and Religious Classics of East and West*, no. 20.) [With a bibliography, and a study of the evolution of the Barlaam and Josaphat legend in oriental literature.]
LEROY, J. 'Un nouveau manuscrit arabe-chrétien illustré du Roman de Barlaam et Joasaph', in *Syria*, XXXII, 1955, pp. 101-22.
MANSELLI, Raoul. 'The Legend of Barlaam and Joasaph in Byzantium and in the Romance Europe', in *East and West*, VII, no. 4, Rome, 1957, pp. 331-40.
MARR, N. Ya. 'Agiograficheskie materialy po gruzinskim rukopisyam Ivera' ('Hagiographical materials from Georgian manuscripts on Mount Athos'), 2 pt., in *Zapiski Vostochnago Otdeleniya Imp. Russkago Arkheologicheskago Obshchestva* ('Bulletin of the Oriental Division of the Imperial Russian Archaeological Society'), tom. 13, St Petersburg, 1901.
——'Armyansko-gruzinskie materialy dlya istorii Dushepoleznoy Povesti o Varlaame i Ioasafe' ('Armenian and Georgian materials for the history of the edifying tale of Barlaam and Ioasaph'), in *Zapiski Vostochnago Otdeleniya, etc.*, tom. 11, St Petersburg, 1897-8, pp. 49-78.

SELECT BIBLIOGRAPHY

——"Mudrost' Balavara", gruzinskaya versiya "Dushepoleznoy Istorii o Varlaame i Ioasafe" ('The Wisdom of Balavar, a Georgian version of the edifying story of Barlaam and Ioasaph'), in *Zapiski Vostochnago Otdeleniya, etc.*, tom. 3, St Petersburg, 1889, pp. 223-60.

MILINDA (MENANDER), King. *Milinda's Questions*, Vol. 1. Trans. I. B. Horner, London, 1963. (Sacred Books of the Buddhists. Vol. 22.)

NUTSUBIDZE, Shalva. *K proiskhozhdeniyu grecheskogo romana 'Varlaam i Ioasaf'* ('On the origin of the Greek romance of Barlaam and Ioasaph'), Tbilisi, 1956.

PEETERS, Paul. 'La première traduction latine de "Barlaam et Joasaph" et son original grec', in *Analecta Bollandiana*, XLIX, 1931, pp. 276-312.

PERI (PFLAUM), Hiram. 'Der Religionsdisput der Barlaam-Legende, ein Motiv abendländischer Dichtung', Salamanca, 1959. (*Acta Salmanticensia*, etc., tom. XIV, no. 3.) [With a bibliography, pp. 223-62, of 378 items.]

QAUKHCHISHVILI, Simon. *Bizantiuri literaturis istoria*. ('History of Byzantine literature'), Tbilisi, 1963.

REHATSEK, E., trans. 'The Book of the King's Son and the Ascetic', in *Journal of the Royal Asiatic Society*, 1890, pp. 119-55.

RHYS DAVIDS, T. W., trans. *Buddhist Birth-Stories* (Jataka Tales), revised edition, London, 1925.

ROSEN, Viktor R., trans. *Povest' o Varlaame pustynnike i Iosafe tsareviche indiyskom*, [translated from the Bombay Arabic version and published posthumously] under the editorship of I. Yu. Krachkovsky, Moscow, 1947.

RUNCIMAN, Sir Steven. *The Medieval Manichee. A Study of the Christian Dualist Heresy*, Cambridge, 1947.

TARCHNIŠVILI (TARKHNISHVILI), Michael. 'Les deux recensions du "Barlaam" géorgien', in *Le Muséon*, LXXI, Louvain, 1958, pp. 65-86.

——'Le roman de Balahvar et sa traduction anglaise', in *Orientalia Christiana Periodica*, XXIV, no. 1-2, Roma, 1958, pp. 83-92.

WOLFF, R. L. 'The Apology of Aristides—A Re-examination', in *Harvard Theological Review*, XXX, 1937, pp. 233-47.

——'Barlaam and Ioasaph', in *Harvard Theological Review*, XXXII, 1939, pp. 131-9.

WOODWARD, G. R. and H. MATTINGLY, edit. and trans. *Barlaam and Ioasaph*, London, 1914, etc. (Loeb Classical Library.)

ZOTENBERG, H. 'Notice sur le livre de Barlaam et Joasaph', in *Notices et extraits des mss. de la Bibliothèque Nationale*, XXVIII, Paris, 1886.

INDEX

Abenes (Abenner), king of India, derivation of his name, 37; withstood by Iodasaph, 44; redeemed, 46; his original wickedness, 53; persecutes the Christians, 54; birth of his son, Iodasaph, 59; builds a separate palace for Iodasaph, 60; allows him to ride outside, 67; learns of Iodasaph's conversion, 122; murders a band of hermits, 127; reasons with Iodasaph, 128; arranges a mock debate on the faith, 137; welcomes the pagan hermit Thedma, 142; tempts Iodasaph with beautiful girls, 145; divides his kingdom with Iodasaph, 149; converted to Christianity, 163; surrenders his entire realm, 165; repents and dies, 170
Abukura, trans. by Euthymius the Iberian, 40
Abuladze, Professor I. V., 12-13, 79, 96, 99
Adish Gospels, 32
Ahmadiyya movement in Islam, 11
Albigensians, medieval sect, 9
Antwerp, 9
Arabian Nights, 90
Arabs, Arabic, 11-13, 20-21, 24, 27, 28-30, 32-4, 36-9, 44, 53, 64, 71, 78, 86, 88, 90-91, 96, 135
Araches, see Rakhis
Aristides, Apology of, inserted into the Greek redaction, 32, 139
Armenia, Armenian language, 33, 39
Armenian version of Barlaam romance, 21
Arsenius, Epistles of, 34
Athos, Mount, 12

Baghdad, 90
al-Bahwan, a heathen sorcerer, see Thedma
Baisam, King, 135
Balahvar, a holy hermit, hears of Iodasaph's desire for enlightenment, 44, 71; arrives from Sarandib, 71; gains entry to the palace, 73;

preaches to Iodasaph in parables, 73-97; describes his ascetic way of life, 113-16; exchanges garments with Iodasaph, 117; takes leave of him, 119-20; hunted in vain by King Abenes, 123; rejoined by Iodasaph, 178; dies in holiness, 179
Barakhia, a Christian; Iodasaph's friend in time of need, 128; attends the mock debate, 137; chosen by Iodasaph to succeed him as king of India, 172; declines but is obliged to accept, 174; recovers the relics of Balahvar and Iodasaph, 180
Barlaam, a holy hermit, see Balahvar
Belial, 43, 47
Beridze, Professor Vakhtang, 17
Bilauhar, see Balahvar
Blake, Professor Robert P., 23, 26, 34
Bodhisattva, 9-13
Boissonade, J. F., 19
Bombay, 21
Boyce, Prof. Mary, 12, 34-5, 88, 127
Buddha, Gautama, 9-13, 19, 69, 89
Budhasaf (Bodisav, Budasaf), see Iodasaph
Burton, Sir Richard, 90-91
Byzantine Christianity, 13
Byzantine literature, 26, 40

Cairo, refuse mounds near, 91
Caliphs of Baghdad, 'Abbasid, 20
Cathars, medieval sect, 9
Caucasian Iberia, 33
Caucasus, 12
Central Asia, 11-12, 20, 88
Ceylon (Sarandib), 29, 71, 178
Chita, Georgian scribe, 101
Ctesiphon, 27

David, King of Israel, 45, 147
David, Georgian scribe, 70, 92, 100, 121, 170, 178
Der Nersessian, Professor S., 17
Devos, P., Bollandist scholar, 25
Doge of Venice, 9
Dölger, Professor Franz, 25

INDEX

Elias, the Prophet, 47
Ethiopia, 11
Euthymius, Saint, the Georgian, translator of the Barlaam romance, 12, 22, 30, 38-40

al-Fihrist, Kitab, 21
Filantin, King, 135
Filliozat, J., 64
Foley, Mr Tom, 10
Four Omens, 9, 69

Garitte, Professor G., 13, 25, 34
George, Saint, the Hagiorite, 37, 39-40
Giorgi, see George
Great Renunciation, of Gautama Buddha, 10
Greece, Greek, 33, 36-41
Grégoire, Professor Henri, 25

Halkin, Father F., Bollandist scholar, 25
Harun al-Rashid, Caliph, 11, 90
Henning, Professor W. B., 12, 88, 89
Hommel, F., 21, 22

Iberia, Caucasian, 33
Iceland, 11
Idols, Idolatry, 96-7, 137-44, 163-6
India, Indians, 9-11, 19, 37, 43, 53, 64, 121, 153
Ioasaph, see Josaphat
Iodasaph (Ioasaph, Josaphat), Saint, Prince of India, derivation of his name, 29; hymn to, 43-50; his birth, 59; prediction that he will be a holy man, 60; confined in a palace apart, 60; his intelligence and merit, 65; pines to leave the palace, 66; sallies forth and sees deformed and senile men, 68; frets and repines, 69-70; welcomes the holy Balahvar, 73; listens to his preaching and parables, 73-116; exchanges garments with Balahvar, 117; fasts and prays, 121; argues with King Abenes, 128-37; emerges victorious from mock debate on the faith, 141; tempted by women, 145-8; accepts half of his father's realm, 152; excels as a ruler, 157; converts his father Abenes, 163; rejoins Balahvar in the wilderness, 178; dies in holiness, 180

Iran, Iranians, 20, 33-5

Janaisar (Abenes), king, 37, 135
Janashvili, M., 23
Javakhishvili, Professor I. A., 22, 34
Jerusalem, 13, 23, 26, 43, 79, 87
Jesuits, turn Barlaam story into plays, 9
Jghamaia, Ts., 37, 43
John the Baptist, Saint, 47
John of Damascus, Saint, 25, 41
Josaphat, see Iodasaph

Kashmir, 11
Kekelidze, Professor K. S., 20, 27-30, 36, 40
Khakhanov, Professor A. S., 23
Khusrau Anushirvan, King, 20
King, Winston L., book on Buddhism criticized, 11
Kitab Bilauhar wa-Budasaf, 12, 21, 32, 36, 64, 135
Krachkovsky, Professor I. Yu., 20

Lalita-vistara, 19
Latin version of Barlaam romance, 21
Leroy, Father Jules, 17
Library of Congress, 26
Limonarion, 26
Logothetes, Simeon, called the Metaphrast, 30
Louvain, University of, 13
Lucifer, Prince of Darkness, 45

Mani, Manichaeans, 11-12, 13, 88-9, 125
Marr, Academician N.Y., 22-4, 29, 40-41
Merchant of Venice, The, 9
Metaphrastes, Simeon, 30
Michael the Sabaite, Saint and Martyr, 40
Michael, Georgian monk, 120
Michael, Georgian scribe, 159, 178
Migne, Abbé J.P., 19
Moschus, John, 26

al-Nadim, Arabic bibliographer, 21
Nakhor, a pagan hermit and sorcerer, in features like Balahvar, 123, 127-8, 137-41
Nestorian Church, 20, 27
Nikordsminda, church at, 17
Nutsubidze, Professor Shalva, 25-6, 27

Omens, the Four, 9, 69

Parthia, Parthian, 34, 127
Paul, Saint and Apostle, 173
Peeters, Father Paul, 24, 34
Pehlevi (Iranian) language and script, 20-21, 29, 33-5
Persia, Persian, 12, 33-5
Philippines, 11
Poland, 11
Prochorus, Saint, the Georgian, 120

Qaukhchishvili, Professor Simon, 26, 58, 96

Rakhis, chief counsellor of King Abenes, derivation of his name, 29; his wily ruses, 122-3; catches a group of ascetics, 124; arranges mock debate on the faith, 127, 137
Ratcha, district of Georgia, 13, 17
Rosen, Baron V. R., 20, 22, 64
Runciman, Sir Steven, 125

Saba, cloister of Saint, 40
Saba, Georgian monk, 120
Salvator, church of Saint, in Antwerp, 9
Sarandib (Ceylon), 29, 71, 178
Satan, 90, 104, 135
Sebastian, King of Portugal, 9
Seleucia, 27
Senaar, 29

Shabakhna, King, 135
Shakespeare, William, 9
Shawilabat, see Sholait
Sholait, 29, 53
Simeon Logothetes, surnamed the Metaphrast, 30
Syria, Syriac language, 20, 24, 27-8, 33, 39

Talzin, King, 135
T'aqaishvili, Professor E., 22
Tarkhnishvili, Father Michael, 25, 32-5
Tbilisi (Tiflis), 12-13
Thedma (Theudas), a notable sorcerer, 29; exposes Iodasaph to temptation, 142-5; converted to Christianity, 165-8
Thomas, Saint and Apostle, 28, 153
Tolstoy, Count Leo, 9-10
Tsereteli, Professor Giorgi, 13
Turkish language, 20

Venice, Doge of, 9

Wolff, Professor R. L., 24

Yuz Asaf, 11

Zadan, tutor to Iodasaph, 110-12, 121-2
Zangwill, Israel, 7
Zoroaster, Zoroastrianism, 89
Zotenberg, H., 21-2, 25

For Product Safety Concerns and Information please contact our EU representative GPSR@taylorandfrancis.com
Taylor & Francis Verlag GmbH, Kaufingerstraße 24, 80331 München, Germany

www.ingramcontent.com/pod-product-compliance
Lightning Source LLC
Chambersburg PA
CBHW061835300426
44115CB00013B/2385